Break-Through is the story of thousands of small groups—Bible cells, Bible study circles, discipleship classes, or whatever you want to call them. We are shown many examples of how they work and the varied methods used to study the Bible.

Mr. Rees also gives practical instructions on how to start a group, how to lead one, the mechanics involved, the spiritual responsibility entailed. Important directions also include warnings about what not to do. And there are suggestions for spiritual growth through seven spiritual disciplines.

About the author

Tom Rees's ministry has taken him to every one of the 50 countries in the British Isles and the 10 Canadian Provinces, as well as many places in the United States. He has been in evangelistic work for the past 40 years. Since 1945 his ministry has been centered in Hildenborough Hall, a big country estate in Kent, which is used as an inter-church training center for young people. Mr. Rees and his wife Jean, who is an accomplished speaker and writer herself, have two children, Jennifer and Justyn, both of whom are married.

BREAK-THROUGH

by

Tom Rees

WORD BOOKS, *Publisher*
Waco, Texas

Break-through

And they come unto Him, bringing one sick of the palsy, and
they sought means to bring him in, and to lay him before
Him. And when they could not find by what way they might
bring him in because of the multitude, they went upon the
housetop, and *when they had broken it up,* they let him down
through the tiling with his couch before Jesus.

– Matthew 9, Mark 2, Luke 5

I kept back nothing that was profitable unto you, but have
shewed you, and have taught you publickly, *and from house
to house,* testifying both to the Jews, and also to the Greeks,
repentance toward God, and faith toward our Lord Jesus
Christ.

– St. Paul to the Ephesians

TO MY FRIENDS

STEPHEN AND HEATHER OLFORD

OF NEW YORK CITY

ACKNOWLEDGMENTS

MY warmest thanks to all those who have helped in the writing and production of this book – to my wife Jean, my friend Annie Vallotton the artist, my secretary Joyce Silcox, Stanley Alexander, Donald Guthrie, Edward Smith, Bill Smyly, and John Taylor.

I am particularly indebted to the American Bible Society for their generosity in permitting their specially commissioned illustrations by Annie Vallotton to be included in this book. These drawings were copyrighted by the Society in 1966, and in no circumstances can they be reproduced without special permission.

TOM REES

Contents

THE subject-matter of this book does not lend itself to the usual chapter divisions. A comprehensive Index of Subjects will be found at the end of the book. In broad outline the contents are as follows:

Illustrations by Annie Vallotton

8

An Explosive Break-through

HERE in Britain since the first world war there has been an ever increasing falling away from organised religion. Since the second world war this has become a landslide. Every year hundreds of churches are closing down, congregations are amalgamating, and each of the historic denominations report declining membership, and all this in the face of an unprecedented population explosion.

One of our largest Protestant denominations recently appointed a Commission to discover the reason why their membership was declining so rapidly, and why so many of their ministers were leaving to find employment in other professions. Their findings have not yet been published, but a member of this Commission, a personal friend of mine, told me that he and his colleagues have already come to the conclusion that (apart from a miracle) in less than twenty-five years their denomination will be completely extinct.

The vicar of a large industrial parish, who, before his ordination, spent much of his life working on the factory floor, tells me: "The British working man has no time for the Church, or the parson. However, he is still deeply interested in God, the world to come, and – provided he can find someone to explain it to him – the Bible."

To enlightened people three facts stand out clearly. One, we Christians have, in the Bible, God's message for the world. Two, the people of our generation, including our immediate relatives and neighbours, are in desperate need of the message entrusted to us. Three, we are faced today with what seems to be an almost insuperable problem: the means of communicating that message. Between committed Christians on the one hand, and the godless, unchurched multitudes on the other, there is an insurmountable wall of partition. The two live and move in isolated worlds. We are like physicians who, living in a plague-infested city, hold ample supplies of a sure remedy, but have no means of telling their sick fellow citizens the news of the certain cure.

Here in England our churches are virtually empty; it is estimated that ninety-four people out of every hundred seldom, if ever, enter a church. Mass evangelism, although effective in helping 'fringe' people, leaves 'the man in the street' largely untouched. Those on the broad and easy way neither hear nor read the message of Life through church, crusade, radio, TV, book, or personal witness.

Joel, a disciple of Jesus, was deeply concerned about his neighbour who was helplessly paralysed, so he called together three friends who, like himself, each had a strong personal faith in Christ, and he told them of the grievous spiritual and physical needs of his sick friend. The four of them agreed that the Lord Jesus, and He alone, could forgive and heal the palsied man; but there was one enormous problem: how could their bedridden neighbour get to the feet of Jesus? (Means of communication are no modern problem!) As they prayed together, the answer came! Were they not all strong, able-bodied men? Then they would carry their neighbour, bed and all, and put him right down at the Master's feet! But their difficulties were by no means over. Having heard that the Master was teaching in a private home, they found the doors and the windows surrounded with an inquisitive mob who were neither wanting salvation for themselves, nor were willing to make way for the helpless man to be brought to the Master's feet. What were Joel and his three fellow stretcher-bearers to do? Give up and take their friend back to his despairing wife and family? "No," said Joel, "only yesterday I heard the Master say that if we have faith, we can remove mountains. . . . Yes, I've got it, the answer is BREAK-THROUGH!"

And they come unto Him, bringing one sick of the palsy, which was borne of four . . . and they sought means to bring him in, and to lay him before Him. And when they could not find by what way they might bring him in because of the multitude, they went upon the housetop, and *when they had broken it up,* they let him down through the tiling with his couch into the midst before Jesus.

And Jesus seeing their faith said unto the sick of the palsy; Son, be of good cheer; thy sins be forgiven thee. – Matthew 9, Mark 2, Luke 5.

Yes, it was *'Operation Break-through'* carried out by the faith and vision of Joel and his three fellow disciples which brought forgiveness of sin, and newness of life to their neighbour and his family.

Break-through! Yes, thank God, in the midst of this alarming fall-away from organised religion, a new and exciting thing is taking place – the most exciting and significant thing that has happened in the spiritual world since the 18th century – common people are meeting regularly in one another's homes to pray, and read the Bible, and are discovering for themselves exactly what the Christian gospel is, which 2,000 years ago turned the world upside down. Yes, and these groups are an explosive break-through into the homes and hearts of multitudes who are without God, or hope. Countless individuals and whole families are finding forgiveness of sin and new life in Christ. For every church that closes down, ten new Bible Cells spring up.

In different generations God works in various ways. In the 18th century He spoke through the open air preaching of John Wesley and George Whitefield, in the last twenty-five years He has been speaking through great Crusades, but unless I am mistaken, today He is speaking mainly to people in their homes.

A short while ago people had to go out to the cinema, or the theatre, to see a film or a play; today they watch in their own homes. Until recently people had to go out to church, or to a crusade to hear the Word of God, but today, with open Bibles, they hear God's Word in their own homes. What hath God wrought!

That pernicious religion of communism – and make no doubt about it, communism *is* a religion – has spread its poisonous doctrine to the ends of the earth, not so much by mass media, but rather by innumerable small 'cells' of men and women, each of whom is completely dedicated to one task: the conquest of the world by communism. These cells, carefully organised and rigidly disciplined, are placed strategically in our colleges, schools, factories, government offices, etc. When a cell becomes large or popular, it is immediately divided or subdivided.

I asked an authority on communism to tell me how these cells worked, and the secret of their success. "The answer is simple," he said. "Each cell has but three rules, and to these rules each member is fully committed. (1) Know your doctrine. (2) Keep in daily touch with Headquarters. (3) Have a strategic, effective plan for making converts."

Augustine once described the devil as 'God's monkey', because the devil copies everything God seeks to do. Communism is both the very image and the very antithesis of New Testament Christianity. Each morning at sunrise in the great communist youth camps thousands of disciplined young people salute the red flag, and cry: "Lenin lived; Lenin lives; Lenin always will live" – and what is this but an ugly caricature of the creed of the New Testament Church? And what is the technique of the modern communist cell, but a copy of the strategic plan for evangelism laid down by our Lord, and practised by His Apostles and the New Testament Church, who:

1. knew their doctrine, and were ready always to give an answer (from the Scriptures) as to why they believed and behaved as they did – 1 Peter 3: 15.
2. were in daily touch with Headquarters, walking in living fellowship with their risen Lord by the Word of God, prayer, faith, and obedience – Acts 2: 42–47.
3. had a God-given, strategic and effective plan for making new converts among their neighbours by going from house to house gossiping the good news of Christ – Acts 8: 4; 20: 20.

Few laymen have more sympathy with Christian ministers than I, and few believe in mass evangelism more than I. The public proclamation of the Word of Life must continue both through the local church and the large crusade, but at this critical hour God is working particularly through innumerable small groups meeting 'from house to house'. This is the work of God, and I for one am anxious to be deeply involved in what God is doing.

It is my earnest prayer that this book be used to the formation of many new Bible Cells, and the inspiration and instruction of those already formed.

TOM REES

Hildenborough Hall,
Otford Hills, Sevenoaks,
Kent, England.

The Finger of God

In the years 1958 and 1961 I conducted two missions on a national scale – the Mission to Britain when, after a commissioning service in St. Paul's Cathedral, we travelled over 10,000 miles in seven months visiting 158 centres of population in every county in Great Britain and Northern Ireland, from Land's End to John O' Groats, from Londonderry to Dover. The other, the Mission to Canada, when, after being commissioned by the leaders of the historic Protestant Churches, we travelled by rail, road and air 24,000 miles, and covered the ten Provinces of the Dominion from St. John's, Newfoundland, to Whitehorse in the Yukon. I averaged 300 miles' travel, and preached three times each day for five months non-stop. During these two national missions we saw many hundreds turning to Christ. In practically every city and town we visited, both in Britain and Canada, I held conferences for ministers – often every Protestant minister in the area was present – and again and again I was asked the same question: "Do you see any signs of a genuine spiritual awakening in the English-speaking world?" and in all honesty I was compelled to answer "No", and this, in spite of the fact that 'mass' evangelism was very much in vogue at that time – Billy Graham's great crusades in Harringay, in Glasgow, and – on a smaller scale – our own meetings in London's Royal Albert Hall. Obviously there is a world of difference between successful evangelism and widespread spiritual awakening. Today when in my various travels I am asked the same question, I have, thank God, a very different answer: "Undoubtedly yes! 'There is a sound of a going in the tops of the mulberry trees', a most significant moving of God's Spirit . . ." and then I tell of the spiritual phenomenon of the Bible Cells and of the miracles that God is working in them and through them.

Today, wherever I travel, in city and country alike a most remarkable thing is taking place – certainly the most significant thing I have ever seen – something which is neither organised nor promoted – advertised nor publicised – something which is not the work of man, but beyond doubt the very hand of God. Christian people are spontaneously opening their homes to their neighbours, and are seeking God by reading the Bible and praying together, and everywhere miracles are taking place, not only in the lives of Christian people, but also amongst those who never go to church, or take any interest in spiritual things.

This phenomenon is by no means limited to Britain: I have attended scores of these meetings both in the United States and Canada, and reports are coming in from countries all over the world. Nor is this movement limited to any social or educational group. An Anglican rector in the East End of London tells me of the thrilling miracles that are taking place amongst his under-privileged people, and similar miracles are being performed in our universities.

Since I became a Christian I have read innumerable books telling thrilling stories of great evangelical revivals of the past, and seldom a day has passed without my asking God to visit us in our generation with just such a movement of His Spirit; but although from time to time I have seen God at work in local communities, I have never yet seen widespread spiritual awakening. This deep desire for revival is, I know, shared by many of my fellow Christians throughout the world, but I wonder if we are not mistaken in our ideas as to how God will answer our prayers – as to the means He might use, and the form that the revival might take. Perhaps whilst we envisage crowded churches, God is moving 'from house to house', and whilst we dream of God raising up another White-field or Finney, He is seeking to work through common people like ourselves. I believe that if only we were sensitive to the way in which God is working, we would open our hearts and our homes to our neighbours, and discover that revival is with us here and now in our very midst.

> And when David enquired of the Lord, He said, Thou shalt not go up; but fetch a compass behind them, and come upon them over against the mulberry trees. And let it be, when thou hearest the sound of a going in the tops of the mulberry trees, that then thou shalt bestir thyself: for then shall the Lord go out before thee, to smite the host of the Philistines. – 2 Samuel 5: 23, 24.

BIBLE CELLS

The names by which these Home Groups are known are legion: Bible Study Circles – Prayer Groups – Bible Breakfasts – Bible Coffee Mornings – Discipleship Classes – Christian Study Units – to name but a few.

The name that appeals to me most is one that I came across in the States – Bible Cells. Of course, the word 'cell' here does not refer to a monk's bedroom, or an apartment occupied by those

enjoying the Queen's hospitality! It is used in the sense of a living cell – 'the ultimate element of a living structure'!

A seed consists largely of living cells which will, if the seed is germinated, grow, divide, subdivide, develop, and finally produce fruit and seed after its kind. And for this reason the Master likened the Scriptures to seed.

The *seed* is the Word of God. – Luke 8: 11.

And the Apostle Peter also took up the simile:

Being born again, not of corruptible *seed*, but of incorruptible, by *the Word of God*, which liveth and abideth for ever. . . . But *the Word of the Lord* endureth for ever. And this is *the Word* which by *the gospel* is preached unto you. – 1 Peter 1: 23, 25.

The seed is the Word of God

Bible Cells! No, the Word of God is not dead and ineffective, but 'quick and powerful' – living and active (Hebrews 4: 12), and when the seed of its message is sown in the hearts and minds of those who will hear and understand, divine life and fruit are the inevitable result. Bible Cells! I like that! And with your permission, Mr. Reader, this is the name that I shall use to describe these groups which gather together in private homes to pray and study the Word – Bible Cells.

But whatever happens, don't let's get bogged down with denominations – names – call these groups what you will – the thrilling and vital thing is this: God is at work!

A NOTABLE MIRACLE

Let me tell you about one of the many miracles which are taking place. I was there when it happened.

A Christian farmer and his wife invited some of their friends to a Tuesday evening Bible Study in their farm kitchen, and after a few weeks of reading and praying together, they found themselves thinking about their non-Christian neighbours. Thought led to prayer. They started praying, not vaguely, but specifically, praying for people and families by name. Major and Mrs. Mander, the farmer and his wife, started praying particularly for Mr. and Mrs. Tedder who live in the village; he is a painter and decorator and runs his own business. But by and by prayer led to concern. The Christian group stopped thinking of their neighbours merely as 'worldly people', or even as 'souls to be won' and started to see them as men and women in desperate need – a need of which, alas, they were often quite unaware. This concern in turn led to action. No, this action did not take the form of giving out tracts, or inviting the neighbours to hear the gospel (this came much later). The first action of this Bible Cell was that of showing practical human kindness, or should I say Christian kindness? The Manders wondered how they could show the kindness of God to the Tedders. They did not have to wait very long.

Before I go any further I must tell you a little more about the Tedders. Although Charles and Ruth were married in church, they were completely ignorant of spiritual things. They saw no more beauty in Christ than a blind man sees in a rainbow, and they appreciated the Bible no more than a deaf man does an orchestra. Every Sunday, except when the weather was bad, they packed the three children into the car, and headed for the sea.

Now, soon after the Manders started concentrating their prayers and faith on the Tedder family, God started to work, and, as He often does, He started through a child. One wet Sunday eleven-year-old Jeremy Tedder, with some hesitation, accepted an invitation to go to a Bible Class, and to his surprise he thoroughly enjoyed himself. The leader of that class loves both God and small boys! Not long afterwards, one night Charles went up to say 'goodnight' to Jeremy, and was greatly embarrassed to find the child on his knees saying his prayers. Why ever should a lad of eleven want to pray? But Charles and Ruth were even more mystified later that week.

"Charles," said Ruth, "Young Jeremy has got a Bible from somewhere, and he keeps it at the side of his bed – and he seems to be reading it too!"

THE SWORD OF DIVISION

The following Sunday morning was fine and clear, and as the Tedder family sat down to breakfast father said:

"Come along, let's eat quickly, and make an early start."

"I'm not going to the sea-side today," said young Jeremy.

There was a moment of shocked silence before his father answered.

"Not going? Whatever d'you mean? Of course you're going! We always go out together on Sunday, you know we do! Why don't you want to come? What's the matter with you?"

"I'd rather stay at home and go to Bible Class and church," said Jeremy.

"Bible Class! Church. . . !" said Charles, and then he said a lot more which today he deeply regrets.

So the sword of division had fallen on the Tedder's home! How utterly relevant and up to date the Bible is!

Suppose ye that I am come to give peace on earth? I tell you, Nay; but rather division: For from henceforth there shall be five in one house divided, three against two, and two against three. The father shall be divided against the son, and the son against the father. – Luke 12: 51–53.

Why a lively boy like Jeremy should want to go to church, read the Bible, and pray was a complete mystery to both Charles and his wife, and yet. . . .

In the meanwhile the Manders, with two or three other members of their Bible Cell, continued praying, waiting, and watching for their moment, or rather for God's moment; and as I say, they didn't have to wait long.

Ruth went down with pneumonia, and a few days later Charles

17

was stricken with a coronary thrombosis, and was ordered to bed for several weeks.

"Who will take care of the children, and how are we going to live if you can't work?" asked Ruth.

News travels quickly in a village! And when Mrs. Mander heard of the Tedders' plight, she did *not* say, "Oh, I am sorry!" Nor did she send a letter of sympathy assuring them of prayer! No! she swung into action! In less than an hour she arrived at the Tedders' home carrying a basket of fresh eggs, milk, beef tea and other goodies, and walked right upstairs into the bedroom.

"There's nothing to worry about. Charles is going to be all right. I've just been on the phone to the doctor, and he's most reassuring. I called on Mrs. Hastings on my way, and she's coming in to nurse you – and as for the children – they're coming to stay at the farm till you're better – they love it up there. I'll pick them up when they come out of school. . . ."

Later that night when the three excited Tedder children were safely tucked up in bed at Warren Farm, and the members of the Bible Cell gathered downstairs in the big kitchen, Major Mander said:

"Mrs. Hastings will not be able to come tonight, as she is looking after Ruth Tedder. . . ."

THE PRAYER COVENANT

And then he and his wife took the group into their confidence and told them how for many months they had been praying for the Tedder family. It was unanimously agreed that the group would pray privately every day, and unitedly each week, that through this sickness the Tedders would find new life in Christ.

The next day Mrs. Mander called on her minister, a real man of God, and enlisted his prayer support too, but – and this is very important – the Manders, the minister, and the Bible Cell not only prayed, but they also lavished their love and generosity upon the Tedders – parents and children alike. Moreover, no one throughout this critical time quoted a text, or left a religious book for Charles and Ruth to read – such an action would have been laying the snare in the sight of the bird.

Yes, the Warren Farm Cell were really learning how to love and win people, and where had they learned this? Some while before, they had studied a series of selected passages in the first Epistle of John, and God had spoken to them of their responsibility to their neighbours.

If any one has the world's goods and sees his brother in

Love not in word, but in deed

need, yet closes his heart against him, how does God's love abide in him? Little children, let us not love in word or speech but in deed and in truth. – 1 John 3: 17, 18. R.S.V.

Yes, the Tedders were surrounded by prayer, faith, practical kindness, and genuine Christian love – capitulation was inevitable!

Ruth and Charles both made a good recovery, and those black days of anxiety faded from their minds like an ugly dream, but one thing they never forgot – the loving kindness of the Manders, Mrs. Hastings, and the minister. Was it just a coincidence that all those people were 'religious'? But in the meanwhile at Warren Farm prayer was made without ceasing unto God for them.

One Tuesday morning Mrs. Mander was constrained to invite both Charles and Ruth to an open Bible Study they were having that night. How irregular! The Bible is for enlightened Christian people! Whatever could people like the Tedders get out of it! Surely they'll spoil the atmosphere! Take them to church, or to a crusade, yes, but to a Bible Study? Surely not! Yes, by all means! One of the most exciting things about the Bible Cells is just this – non-christian people are coming to study the Bible and to pray, and as a result are turning to Christ! The Bible itself, illuminated by the Holy Spirit, makes people wise unto salvation not only when its message is preached from the pulpit, but when it is read and studied personally by needy folk whose hearts have been prepared by prayer, but more about this later.

Of course, the Tedders tried to wriggle out of Mrs. Mander's invitation:

"It's very kind of you. Charles and I would love to come, but of course we just cannot leave the children."

Mrs. Mander was ready for that one too!

"I've thought of that, and have already arranged a baby sitter for you."

And so she had! There was just no escape for Charles and Ruth, so they went, or rather they came, for I was there that night when the dead were raised.

THE BIBLE AT WORK

There were about fifteen of us at the Warren Farm that night – an ideal number I thought. It was clear to me that these folk, drawn from different Church backgrounds, knew each other well, and loved each other dearly. Most of them were married couples whose ages ranged from about thirty to sixty-five. We started with a cup of tea and general conversation, broken by a good deal of natural merriment, then we all sat down, including Mr. Thornton whose turn it was to lead the group. Bibles were provided for those who had not brought their own. (Now please forgive me, Mr. Reader, but I am most anxious, for the benefit of other leaders, to describe in some detail exactly how Mr. Thornton guided this verse-by-verse Bible Study, and as you will see this particular meeting transformed the lives of Charles and Ruth.) After welcoming us the leader said:

"Now, before we read the Bible, we are going to ask Mr. Whittaker to lead us in a prayer."

The prayer was short and sweet.

"Now," said Mr. Thornton, "we are going to study the story of how Captain Naaman of Syria was cured of his leprosy. You'll find it in 2 Kings chapter 5."

Charles glanced at his wife in panic – neither of them had a clue where to find 2 Kings, but to their intense relief the leader went right on. . . .

"You'll find the chapter on page 385 in your Bibles."

The Tedders heaved a sigh of relief!

"Now tonight," said the leader, "instead of asking someone to read the chapter to us, I thought that by way of a change we would read alternate verses. I'll read the first verse and you the second, and so on. If you are not using the King James' Authorised Version you had better not join in. We will finish reading at the end of verse nineteen. When you have all found the place, before we read there are one or two things which I have looked up which I should like to share with you. I only want three minutes, and after that I'm going to let you do the talking."

(Wise man, I thought. Alas, I have seen many similar Bible

Studies wrecked by a leader who would keep preaching and talking!)

Mr. Thornton's comments were brief and to the point.

"The Kingdom of Israel under Jehoram, son of Ahab (he is not named in our chapter) was at this time involved in a cold war with their northern neighbours, the Syrians, whose King was Ben-hadad (his name is not mentioned in our chapter). King Jehoram had his capital in the city of Samaria, whilst Ben-hadad reigned in the ancient city of Damascus. Naaman was Ben-hadad's Field Marshal. Jehoram, although nominally a worshipper of Jehovah, was an apostate king. If you are interested, you can read more about him in 2 Kings chapter 3 when you get home tonight! The King of Syria, his Captain Naaman, and his people were all heathens – worshippers of the God Rimmon. Our chapter tells how, through a healed body, Naaman became a worshipper of the true God.

"To save you embarrassment, earlier today I looked up the correct pronunciation of difficult words which we shall read. The hero's name is Naaman – to rhyme with 'slay a man'. The rivers of Damascus named in verse twelve are Abana – to rhyme with 'banana'. Pharpar – to rhyme with our parents 'Pa Ma'. If you are using the Authorised Version which is printed in the language our ancestors used four centuries ago, there are several old-fashioned words which I should translate. Verse three 'recover' – cure; verse five 'Go to, go' – Go now; verse seven 'rent' – tore (in those days folk deliberately tore the edges of their clothes as a sign of distress); verse eleven 'wroth' – angry; 'recover the leper' – cure the leprosy.

"The verse five refers to 'ten talents of silver, and six thousand pieces of gold'. It is not possible to say how much a talent was worth, or the weight of those pieces of gold, but we can be sure it was worth a fortune, and when Naaman arrived in Samaria he did not have to say to Jehoram what Peter had to say 'Silver and gold have I none'. It was hard for him, as it is for us, to learn that we are not redeemed with corruptible things, as silver and gold."

HOW TO MEDITATE

Then Mr. Thornton continued:

"As we read and study this chapter, look out for answers to the following questions: 'In what way is leprosy a picture of sin?' 'Can you see an example of how God turned a tragedy into a triumph?' 'Can you find an example of effective witnessing?' 'In seeking a cure for the leprosy, both Ben-hadad and Naaman made several mistakes – what were they?' 'What similar mistakes do we make when seeking a cure for our sin?' 'Why didn't Elisha go out and talk to Naaman?' 'What was the real cause of the leper's anger which made him turn away from the prophet's message and the way of recovery?' 'What makes us ignore God's good news to us about forgiveness of sin and new life in Christ? 'Can you see from this story how we should react when we have been made anew by Christ?' 'Can you see here how physical healing should affect our spiritual lives?'

"Now we are going to read this chapter, and as we do so, let us concentrate on what we are reading, and as soon as we are through, I want, for the sake of any newcomers, to give a brief word of explanation as to our method of study."

I glanced at my watch and saw that Mr. Thornton's helpful introductions had lasted exactly three minutes – not too long, yet he had told us all we needed to know. We then read the chapter aloud, slowly and reverently, alternate verses with the leader. This took another three minutes.

"And now," said Mr. Thornton, "We shall go through the chapter paragraph by paragraph. I'll read the verse, then we shall have complete silence whilst we all pray and meditate. First, put up a short, silent prayer such as 'Speak, Lord, for thy servant heareth', then concentrate on the particular verse or verses we are considering. Don't look for sermons for us, but try to discover what God is seeking to say to you. Don't try to criticise the Bible – let it criticise you. Now to help you in your meditation, use the questions set out on the Bible Cell Meditation Card."

It was then that I looked at the card which I had found lying on my chair when I came in and on it were printed the following questions:

What is the main truth of this verse?
What other Scripture can I find to illuminate this verse?
(Look up the margin references given in the Bible)
Is there any word or part of this verse which I do not understand?
Is there a command, or word of advice, here to obey?
Is there a good example to follow?
Is there a sin or mistake to avoid?
Is there a warning to heed?
Is there a promise to claim?
Is there a prayer to echo?
How can I see my own experience reflected here?
How can I apply this Scripture to practical, everyday life?

How can I turn this verse into a prayer?*

"Now after we have had our period of silent prayer and meditation, I want you to tell us (if it's not too personal) just what God has said to you. After that we will take the second verse in a similar manner, and so on. Are you ready then?

"Now Naaman, captain of the host of the king of Syria was a great man with his master, and honourable . . . he was also a mighty man in valour, but he was a leper."

THE LEPROSY OF SIN

The silence that followed was broken only by the tick of the grandfather clock and the rustle of Bible leaves, and as we all prayed and asked God to speak to us personally through His Word, the kitchen of the Warren Farm became the very gate of Heaven. I felt as if I were back in Jerusalem in the house of Mary, the mother of John Mark, where early Christians met for prayer and meditation, and glancing up at Mrs. Mander I understood the true meaning of Apostolic succession!

After about one minute, Mr. Thornton broke the silence.

"All right now, who will start?"

There was no waiting. Major Mander started off:

"I was thinking how this leprosy is just like sin – it's catching. I started to say and do wrong when I was at school just because other boys did it! Leprosy starts in a small way; perhaps Naaman had only a small white spot hidden under his sleeve – yet he was just as much a leper as if he'd been covered with sores. A man is either a leper or he's not, and either I'm a sinner or I'm not – the question is not 'how often have I sinned?' or 'how deeply have I sinned?' but am I, or am I not a sinner? Then again leprosy separates – no one ever went near or touched a leper, except the Lord. Naaman knew that if he could not find a cure, he would be banished from his master, friends, and family. My sin separated me from God for years till I found healing. I thought of those lepers in Luke's Gospel who stood afar off, and what Paul said: 'Ye who sometimes were far off are made nigh by the blood of Christ.' And then of course, leprosy is a killer; there's a verse somewhere which says: 'Sin when it is finished bringeth forth death.' "

There was a moment's silence, then a young woman of about thirty spoke up:

* Copies of this Bible Meditation Card can be obtained price 2s. per dozen (25c) (postage and packing extra) from the Bookroom, Hildenborough Hall, Otford Hills, Sevenoaks, Kent, England.

"It must have been hard for Naaman who was so successful, highly thought of, and had so many good qualities, to face up to the fact that he was a leper; perhaps for some months he kept it quiet and didn't tell anyone. How humiliating for a Field Marshal to contract such a loathsome, fatal disease as leprosy! And then I thought of myself, how a short while ago I started to realise that although I am regarded as a good, respectable, religious person – a good wife and mother and so on, deep in my heart I was a sinner – but I think it was my pride that prevented me from confessing it. If Naaman had not told the King that he was a leper, he would never have been cured. The hardest thing I ever had to do was to kneel down and confess to God that in His sight I was a sinner, and ask Him to cleanse, forgive, and heal me. Some of you here tonight prayed for me at that time, and I feel I owe everything to your prayers. This verse reminded me too of what Jesus said, but I'm sorry I don't know where it comes – 'People who are well don't need the doctor, but those who are ill do!' "

An older man said:

"I was reading that verse only this morning. It's in Matthew chapter 9," and he then read the verse to us.

Charles and Ruth who never went to church, and had refused point blank to go and hear Billy Graham, were now listening spellbound to the Bible, the Gospel, and unrehearsed witnesses, not from the lips of strangers, but from their own neighbours – the very people who had helped to prepare their hearts and minds by earnest prayer and Good Samaritan kindness. The seed was falling into good ground!

CHARLES SPEAKS OUT

Then the leader, Mr. Thornton, spoke up again.

"Yes, everything that has been said so far has been most helpful. Now, let's move on and take verses 2–4 together, since they seem to form a paragraph," and then looking up at a rather shy woman who had not spoken so far, he said: "Mrs. Harris, would you please read the verses to us?"

In quite a pronounced country accent Mrs. Harris read out verses 2–4:

"And the Syrians had gone out by companies, and had brought away captive out of the land of Israel a little maid; and she waited on Naaman's wife. And she said unto her mistress, Would God my lord were with the prophet that is in Samaria! for he would recover him of his leprosy. And one went in, and told his lord, saying, Thus and thus said the maid that is of the land of Israel."

"Thank you," said the leader, "you read that beautifully. I do like to hear the Bible read slowly and thoughtfully. And now, silence once again – don't forget the prayer."

And once more in the stillness of our own hearts we all talked to God and – better still – through His Word, He talked to us.

"Now, who has got something for us?" asked Mr. Thornton.

There was a short silence, and then, shifting nervously in his chair, Charles Tedder spoke up, "Can I say something?"

Ruth glanced at him in surprise, then hastily looked back at her Bible. Mrs. Mander's face was a study. . . .

"At any rate," Charles continued hesitantly, "I hope what I am going to say will be all right, only it's a little difficult. You see, Ruth and I really haven't much idea about Church and the Bible, and God, but a while ago we were both taken ill, and some of you folk were wonderfully kind to us and our children, and that, I think, was the start of it. I don't think we would have done for our neighbours half the things you did for us. Well then, something else happened, and it's only just this minute sitting here looking at these verses have I realised just what it was that did happen, and the significance of it. This Bible seems to be a sort of mirror, because I can see myself in it – I mean I can see my own experience reflected in the experience of Naaman. Let me explain. . . . Naaman's home was not a Christian home, and I'm afraid ours hasn't been either. Now God sent a little child, who loved Him, into Naaman's home, and through her God spoke to Naaman so that he and his family became Christians, or rather they came to know God, and, whilst sitting here I have just come to see that in a similar way God has been speaking to me, and perhaps to my wife, Ruth, here also – through our small son. You see, as I have just said, we are not religious people, and we certainly don't call ourselves Christians. We don't go to church, read the Bible, or say our prayers. Every Sunday, except when the weather's bad, we go down to the sea. Well, something happened to our young Jeremy – something I couldn't understand – not till this minute. He started to say his prayers and read the Bible, and then one Sunday morning he said he wasn't coming out with us, but was going to stay at home, and go to church and Bible Class instead, and then, I'm afraid I got really mad with him. I thought he was just trying to be awkward and spoil our day, but now I can see it clearly. Young Jeremy must have become a Christian – yes, that's what had happened to him, and now I see that just as God sent that little maid into Naaman's home to call him and his wife to

Himself, so God has made my Jeremy into a Christian, and sent him to call me and Ruth to become Christians too. It's all so clear now. . . . And I should just like you all to know that I should really like to become a Christian, and I rather think that that goes for my wife too."

And let me tell you the Angels in Heaven were not the only ones who were rejoicing at that moment! Mrs. Hastings' face was radiant. Mrs. Mander blinked away the tears. Mr. Thornton blew his nose.

Neither of the Tedders took part again that night, but while Charles listened in rapt attention to all that was said, Ruth seemed to be lost in her own thoughts. Once I saw her look up, and in her eyes I saw the reflection of a dawning light.

REPLYING TO GOD

The Bible Study had lasted just over fifty minutes – it seemed more like five to me! Then Mr. Thornton, who had said very little, apart from his introduction, said:

"Now we have just seven minutes left before the hour is up, so I suggest we spend the time by having a number of short prayers – keep them really short please – not general prayers, but prayers which arise from tonight's study."

The prayers that followed were short, natural, and carried the mark of a divine originality. I felt that these people were just talking to God in a similar way in which He had been talking to them – and about the same things too!

"I thank Thee, Lord, for that young Israelite who, when she was taken away as a slave, still trusted in Thee and witnessed for Thee. Help me when things seem to go wrong, to follow her example – Amen."

"O Lord, help me, like Naaman, to overcome my bad temper, which so often like his is caused by my pride—Amen."

"Dear Lord, as the captive maid prayed for the healing of her master, we also pray for those known to us, who are ill at this time, especially for little Joan Reynolds. Lay your hand on her, and use this illness to bring her family to you – Amen."

"We thank Thee Lord for the Gospel, the good news of cleansing and new Life through Christ. We pray that as the leper heard and obeyed the message of the prophet, so may many believe Thy Word wherever it is preached – Amen."

At the end of the seven minutes – exactly one hour after we sat down, Mr. Thornton said:

"Now, I am going to ask Major Mander, our host, to close with a prayer."

His prayer concluded this way.

". . . And now Father, we pray for all those who, like Naaman, are seeking Thee, especially Charles and Ruth Tedder who are here with us this evening. Fulfil Thy promise – those that seek Thee shall find Thee," and to this we all added a heartfelt "Amen". The study hour closed by our saying 'The Grace' together.

NEW CREATURES

And then I noticed a strange thing. People started talking, as they always do after an informal meeting, but these folk did not talk about the weather, the television or their friends – no, they went right on talking about the Lord and His Word, and I thought of the word of the prophet, "They that feared the Lord spake often one to another: and the Lord hearkened, and heard it."

I was sitting in the corner by the grandfather clock next to Mr. Thornton, and almost at once I saw Charles turn and say something to his wife, then they both got up, and came over, and said:

"Mr. Thornton, we've never been to anything like this before. It's all so strange and – different. Could Ruth and I talk to you – privately if possible?"

"Of course," said Mr. Thornton, "let's go through to the dining-room, I am sure Mrs. Mander won't mind."

And during the next half hour the Tedders, guided by their friend, became new creatures. "And his flesh came again like unto the flesh of a little child, and he was clean."

What a welcome Charles and Ruth received from the members of the Warren Farm Bible Cell! They encouraged them, advised them, and loved them. Moreover they taught them how to pray and study the Bible alone, together, and in the fellowship of the Bible Cell – and they also taught them how to witness and win others for Christ – and what apt pupils they were!

We have got to know the Tedders quite well since they became Christians. They have attended several conferences at Hildenborough Hall, but they never come as passengers; they always bring others who are in need, as good working members of the crew.

The Cell at Warren Farm grew too large to be useful, so it was unanimously agreed that they should divide, so now there is another Cell living and growing in the Tedders' home. And what a transformation Christ has made in that home! Charles and Ruth told me recently that they love each other much more since they started loving Christ. The family have prayer together each day – the family that prays together stays together. Charles and Ruth are no longer on the 'receiving' end, but on the giving end. If any one is ill, or in need, the Tedders are there. As the Warren Farm Cell 'covenanted' to pray them into the Kingdom, they too have tasted the thrill of praying for others and seeing them turn to Christ.

Charles doesn't get down to the sea now on Sundays – he is 'otherwise engaged'. He leads a Boys' Bible Class. This involves not only his Sunday afternoon and time for preparation, but on Saturday afternoons he usually takes the lads to a football match.

"If I'm not interested in football on Saturday, then they won't be interested in the lesson on Sunday."

The Master's Method

I HAVE been visiting the U.S.A. and Canada, preaching and teaching since 1936. Recently I made my forty-sixth Atlantic crossing, and have always been interested to notice how people in Britain differ from their American cousins. One of the many contrasts which impresses me is that whereas British people tend to keep themselves to themselves, avoid eating together and visiting one another's homes, folk on the American continent are always getting together, calling on one another, and with the slightest excuse arranging a banquet, luncheon, breakfast, or coffee party. But in the last few years all this has changed. We Britishers have become far more 'Americanised', till today people of every age and walk in life are opening their homes to one another, and are more than happy to visit their neighbours for a meal, a cup of tea, or just for a chat. Some people think that television is largely responsible for this remarkable change, and that may well be, but whatever the reason, the fact is that British people, as never before, are meeting with their neighbours in each other's homes, not reluctantly, but willingly. And this is no doubt one of the reasons for the phenomenal development of Bible Cells throughout Britain. Christian leaders should be sensitive to this change in our social behaviour, and make use of it for the furtherance of the work of God.

Bible Cells are no new innovation. They are as old as the Christian Church itself. Whilst the Master used the open air for mass evangelism,

> There were gathered together an innumerable multitude of people, insomuch that they trode one upon another. – Luke 12: 1.

when He turned to evangelism in depth, to instruction meetings, and the teaching of the twelve, He nearly always used a private home. In the north He set up His headquarters in the home of Simon Peter:

> The same day went *Jesus out of the house*, and sat by the sea side. . . . Then Jesus sent the multitude away, and *went into the house*: and his disciples came unto him. – Matt. 13: 1, 36.

(See also Matthew 8: 14; 17: 22–25 and Mark 9: 28, etc.)

In the south He made His Judaean headquarters in the suburban home of Martha:

> Now it came to pass, as they went, that he entered into a certain village: and a certain woman named Martha *received him into her house.* – Luke 10: 38.

and it is more than likely that it was in this home that Jesus welcomed John and Andrew, and revealed Himself to them as the Christ.

> Then Jesus turned, and saw them following, and saith unto them, What seek ye? They said unto him, Rabbi, (which is to say, being interpreted, Master) *where dwellest thou?* He saith unto them, Come and see. *They came and saw where He dwelt, and abode with him that day*: for it was about the tenth hour. – John 1: 38, 39.

The Son of God was born in a borrowed manger, buried in a borrowed tomb, and did much of His teaching in borrowed homes.

IN MATTHEW'S HOUSE

Matthew (Levi) was a wealthy man who lived in a large house and had plenty of domestic help. Immediately following his conversion he arranged:

> a great feast *in his own house.* – Luke 5: 29.

in the Master's honour, to which he invited his friends and neighbours, and I am fairly certain that he planned this meal at the Master's suggestion.

> And as he passed by, he saw Levi the son of Alphaeus sitting at the receipt of custom, and said unto him, Follow me. And he arose and followed him. And it came to pass, that, *as Jesus sat at meat in his house,* many publicans and sinners sat also together with Jesus and his disciples. – Mark 2: 14, 15.

This feast was arranged not for a 'social evening', but for 'strategic evangelism', to give the great Physician an opportunity of telling sin-sick men the good news of God's remedy for sin. Matthew himself reports the after-dinner speeches – see Matthew 9: 9–13.

The news of Matthew's conversion and his dinner party spread quickly throughout the Publican's Fraternal, and reaching Jericho, aroused the curiosity of his colleague, Zacchaeus (Luke 19: 1–10) who:

> sought to see Jesus who he was; and could not for the press, because he was little of stature. And he ran before, and climbed up into a sycamore tree to see him: for he was to pass that way. – Luke 19: 3, 4.

Today I must abide at thy house

In spite of being rich and successful Zacchaeus was discontented, and was desperately anxious to see Jesus of Nazareth Who had transformed the life of his fellow publican, Matthew. He nearly fell out of the tree with surprise and embarrassment for:

> when Jesus came to the place, he looked up, and saw him, and said unto him, Zacchaeus, make haste, and come down; for today I must abide at thy house. And he made haste, and came down, and received him joyfully. – Luke 19: 5, 6.

D. L. Moody, commenting on this verse once said, "When Zacchaeus let go the branch he was not converted, but before his feet touched the ground he was – sounds like sudden conversion to me!"

But exactly why did Jesus say to Zacchaeus "Today I must abide at thy house?" He had not said anything like this to the blind beggar whose eyes He had opened less than an hour before. Did the Master want a sumptuous meal and a luxurious bed? I don't think so, He was never concerned about his own comfort. No, the plain fact was this: He wanted to use the large and hospitable home of Zacchaeus for the purpose of strategic evangelism. The Master wants not only our hearts, but our homes. As Zacchaeus and his Guest retraced their steps from the sycamore tree, the Master explained what He had in mind, and immediately Zacchaeus set his servants to work preparing food, laying the tables, calling on his relatives and rich neighbours, inviting them to the feast which he was giving that night in honour of Jesus of Nazareth; and what a feast it was!

AFTER DINNER SPEECHES

After dinner, the speeches were made. First, the host himself told of the transformation that the Lord had made in his own life, changing the covetous man into a philanthropist, and the thief into an honest citizen.

> And Zacchaeus stood, and said; Behold, Lord, the half of my goods I give to the poor; and if I have taken any thing from any man by false accusation, I restore him fourfold. – Luke 19: 8.

and then the Master Himself rose to speak. His message was brief and to the point. He Himself had come not only into the world, but to Jericho to seek out, and to save, lost people like Zacchaeus. The way of salvation was by grace through faith.

And Jesus said unto him, This day is salvation come to this house, forsomuch as he also is a son of Abraham. For the Son of man is come to seek and to save that which was lost. – Luke 19: 9, 10.

And beyond doubt, the Master spoke plainly to the family and neighbours of Zacchaeus about their own salvation, leaving them in no doubt that in His eyes they were either saved or lost.

Why is it that the word 'evangelism' immediately brings to the minds of Christian people either a vast crusade, or a formal exposition of Scripture in Church? The Master met men round the breakfast table: (John 21: 12), at an informal picnic (John 6: 1-11), and at a dinner party (Luke 5: 27-29).

A MODERN LYDIA

Recently a successful business woman became a Christian through the prayers and kindness of a local Bible Cell member. One of the first things she did was to arrange a reception such as I have just described. (I know all about it – she invited me to do the talking!) It was a wonderful evening. The meal was plain, yet beautifully prepared. We had no singing, prayers, or Bible reading, though I did hold my New Testament as I spoke, but when we had finished coffee (by this time, like Isaiah's vision 'the house was filled with smoke') our hostess said a brief word of welcome and witness, and then called on me to speak. I wouldn't have missed that opportunity for anything! There were people there who had not been to church, or any kind of religious meeting, for years. But they listened with rapt attention to 'all the words of this life'. Soon they were asking questions, and better still, several have since found this life for themselves.

SIMON THE LEPER

Simon, one of the wealthy residents of Bethany, a fashionable suburb of Jerusalem, was stricken with leprosy, and it was probably through his neighbour, Martha, that he heard of Jesus Who healed him of this living death. Martha and Simon were not the only people in that community who were indebted to the Lord. A little more than a week before His Crucifixion, news reached Bethany that Jesus was coming, and it was unanimously decided to arrange a supper in the Master's honour. An *ad hoc* committee was hastily formed, and although the meal was to be served in Simon's home, Martha was put in charge of the catering (see

Matt. 26: 6–13 and John 12: 1–11). This happy occasion was mainly a love feast for His disciples, but the Master didn't miss the evangelistic opportunity it afforded Him.

In after-dinner speeches, Lazarus would tell how Christ had raised him from the dead, and Simon would tell the story of his cleansing, but no doubt the final word was given by our Lord Himself.

> Much people of the Jews therefore knew that he was there: and they came not for Jesus' sake only, but that they might see Lazarus also, whom he had raised from the dead. But the chief priests consulted that they might put Lazarus also to death; because that by reason of him many of the Jews went away, and believed on Jesus. – John 12: 9–11.

We must not think that this method of reaching our neighbours is limited to financiers like Matthew and Simon, or 'landed gents' like Barnabas (Acts 4: 36, 37), or career girls like Lydia of Philippi (Acts 16: 12–15).

Recently in London a sixth-form schoolboy became a Christian, and persuaded his parents to give a supper party for sixty of his friends on his 17th birthday. After a 'slap-up supper' and some lively games they all settled down, and Alan gave a brief and effective witness, which was followed by a guest speaker who, for twenty minutes, spoke on 'Christianity – Dope or Dynamite?' Members of Bible Cells all over the world are planning just such gatherings. This is the Master's method. Let's get in now on this exciting job.

Our cathedrals, churches, and chapels are perfectly designed for formal worship, but for Group Bible Study, united prayer, heart warming fellowship, and communicating the gospel, we need the friendly, informal atmosphere of a private home.

Again the Master deliberately chose the comfort of a friend's

The Passover at thy house

private house for His final love feast and tender farewell to His beloved Apostles.

> And he said, Go into the city to such a man, and say unto him, The Master saith, My time is at hand; I will keep the passover *at thy house.* – Matt. 26: 18.

> And ye shall say unto *the goodman of the house,* The Master saith unto thee, Where is *the guest chamber,* where I shall eat the passover with my disciples? – Luke 22: 11.

APOSTOLIC TECHNIQUE

In some circles 'technique' has become almost a dirty word, perhaps because some wrongly concentrate more upon technique than upon the power of the Spirit, forgetting that it is men, not methods, that God uses; nevertheless Christian technique is still of the utmost importance, and no observant reader of the gospel can fail to see that the Lord not only taught His disciples the message they were to proclaim, but also instructed them carefully concerning the technique, or method they were to use in proclaiming that message. Just as He had learnt the carpenter's skill during His years of apprenticeship in Joseph's shop, so He taught His young apprentices what to believe and how to behave – the message they were to proclaim, and the method with which they were to proclaim it. He taught them not only by example, but also by plain precept. Consider, for instance, the detailed instructions He gave them before sending them out to preach (see Matthew 10), and here once again we find Him emphasizing the importance of house meetings:

> And into whatsoever city or town ye shall enter, enquire who in it is worthy; and *there abide till ye go thence. And when ye come into an house,* salute it. And if *the house* be worthy, let your peace come upon it: but if it be not worthy, let your peace return to you. And whosoever shall not receive you, nor hear your words, when ye depart out of *that house* or city, shake off the dust of your feet. – Matt. 10: 11–14.

Did the Master preach in the open air to the multitudes? Then His Apostles did the same (Matt. 13: 1–3; Acts 2: 1–14). Did He hold house instruction meetings for those who had ears to hear? Then they did the same (Matt. 13: 1, 9, 36; Acts 2: 37–47). Did the Master teach and preach in private houses? Then His special messengers did likewise.

And they, continuing daily with one accord in the temple, and breaking bread *from house to house,* did eat their meat with gladness and singleness of heart. – Acts 2: 46.

And daily in the temple, *and in every house,* they ceased not to teach and preach Jesus Christ. – Acts 5: 42.

CORNELIUS' DRAWING-ROOM MEETING

That historic sermon preached by the Apostle Peter, and recorded in Acts 10 – historic, because it was the first formal proclamation of the Gospel to a Gentile congregation – was not preached in the temple or a synagogue, but in the *private home* of Cornelius, the Roman Army Officer (this was also the first meeting of the Officers' Christian Union) who had called together his relatives and fellow officers to hear from Peter words whereby they might be saved.

And they said, Cornelius, the centurion, a just man, and one that feareth God, and of good report among all the nation of the Jews, was warned from God by an holy angel *to send for thee into his house,* and to hear words of thee. . . . And the morrow after they entered into Caesarea. And Cornelius waited for them, and had called together his kinsmen and near friends. . . . And he (Peter) said unto them, Ye know how that it is an unlawful thing for a man that is a Jew to keep company, *or come unto one of another nation;* but God hath shewed me that I should not call any man common or unclean. . . . Immediately therefore I sent to thee; and thou hast well done that thou art come. Now therefore are we all here present before God, to hear all things that are commanded thee of God. – Acts 10: 22, 24, 28, 33.

And the Spirit bade me go with them, nothing doubting. Moreover, these six brethren accompanied me, and *we . entered into the man's house.* – Acts 11: 12.

Now what was this but a New Testament house meeting, and home-based evangelism. One man, who himself was seeking God, inviting relatives and friends to his home to hear a guest speaker. The host, acting also as chairman, concluded his introduction of the speaker with these words:

Now therefore are we all here present before God, to hear all things that are commanded thee of God. – Acts 10: 33.

Then Peter, adapting himself to his pagan audience, proclaimed to them in language they could understand, the very essence of the Gospel, the Lord Jesus anointed, crucified, raised, coming again, and ready to forgive. Yes, it was the same gospel that he had proclaimed some months previously on the Day of Pentecost, but whereas to the Jews in Jerusalem he did little but quote the Scripture, here now to the Gentiles in Caesarea he does not quote one word of Scripture. Since most of us are seeking to win Gentiles for Christ, we should study Acts 10 carefully to learn not only the message we are to preach, but also the method we are to use in presenting it.

Immediately after Peter was released from the Jerusalem prison he did not go to the temple or to a synagogue, but made straight for a Bible Cell meeting held in a private home:

> And when he had considered the thing, he came to *the house of Mary* the mother of John, whose surname was Mark; *where many were gathered together praying.* – Acts 12:12.

THE HOME OF AQUILA AND PRISCILLA

When founding the Church in Philippi, Paul and Silas used the homes of the businesswoman, Lydia, and the town jailer (Acts 16:14–16, 32). In Corinth, having testified in vain to the Jews in the synagogue that Jesus was the Christ, he used the private home of his host and hostess, Aquila and Priscilla, and that of Justus with remarkable success:

> After these things Paul departed from Athens, and came to Corinth; and found a certain Jew named Aquila, born in Pontus, lately come from Italy, with his wife Priscilla; (because that Claudius had commanded all Jews to depart from Rome:) and came unto them. And because he was of the same craft, he abode with them, and wrought: for by their occupation they were tent makers. . . . And he departed thence, and entered into *a certain man's house*, named Justus, one that worshipped God, *whose house* joined hard to the synagogue. And Crispus, the chief ruler of the synagogue, believed on the Lord with all his house; and many of the Corinthians hearing believed, and were baptized. – Acts 18:1–3, 7, 8.

And during the next eighteen months he no doubt established many Bible Cells in private homes there in Corinth.

And he continued there a year and six months, teaching the word of God among them. – Acts 18: 11.

When taking his leave of the Ephesian Elders, Paul reminded them not only of the message he had proclaimed, but also of the methods he had used in their midst:

And how I kept back nothing that was profitable unto you, but have shewed you, and have taught you publickly, *and from house to house,* testifying both to the Jews, and also to the Greeks, repentance toward God, and faith toward our Lord Jesus Christ. – Acts 20: 20, 21.

In my various journeys I constantly visit hospitable Christian homes in which Bible Cells flourish under the devoted leadership of a spiritually minded Christian couple who invariably remind me of those warm-hearted friends of Paul, Aquila and Priscilla. These folk were tent makers, and whilst living in Rome they probably became quite wealthy by obtaining various army contracts, but the best thing about them was this – they loved the Lord Jesus, and wherever they lived, they opened their home for a Bible Cell, and in his letter to the Christians in Rome, Paul sent them a special message:

Greet Priscilla and Aquila my helpers in Christ Jesus. . . . Likewise greet *the church that is in their house.* – Romans 16: 3, 5.

After being turned out of Rome with all the other Jews, Aquila and Priscilla lived for a while in Corinth, and when Paul arrived, they entertained him in their home, for they had much in common with the Apostle not only in their occupation, but more especially in their common love for the Lord Jesus. Very soon this godly trio were working together in various homes, leading people to Christ and establishing Bible Cells – and making tents to pay expenses (Acts 18: 18, 19). When the work was well established in Corinth Aquila and Priscilla joined Paul's party and travelled with him to Ephesus where, once again, they established a Bible Cell in their home. Whilst Paul was there in Ephesus he wrote a letter to his converts in Corinth which carried a special greeting from the Ephesian Bible Cells:

The churches of Asia salute you. Aquila and Priscilla salute you much in the Lord, *with the church that is in their house.* – 1 Cor. 16: 19.

What an ideal couple Aquila and Priscilla were! Their hearts and home were always wide open to God's people!

Salute the brethren

When Paul and Timothy wrote to the Christians in Colosse, they asked them to pass on greetings to the Christians in nearby Laodicea, with a special greeting for the Bible Cell which met in the home of Nymphas.

Salute the brethren which are in Laodicea, and Nymphas, and *the church which is in his house.* – Col. 4: 15.

But there was more than one Bible Cell in the city of Colosse, for writing from his prison cell in Rome, Paul addresses a separate letter to another citizen of Colosse, his beloved friend, Philemon, which commences like this:

Paul, a prisoner of Jesus Christ, and Timothy our brother, unto Philemon our dearly beloved, and fellow labourer . . . *and to the church in thy house.* – Philemon 1, 2.

The Church that is *in their house.* – Rom. 16: 5.
The Church that is *in their house.* – 1 Cor. 16: 19.
The Church which is *in his house.* – Col. 4: 15.
The Church *in thy house.* – Philemon 2.

What is the difference between a Bible Cell and a church? Being a mere layman I must leave the answer to ministers and theologians, but of one thing I am certain, if I were a minister, I would do as many are already doing, I would get my people together in small groups, meeting in one another's homes, for Christian fellowship, prayer, Bible Study, and evangelism.

IN HIS OWN HIRED HOUSE

There is always great excitement when a big liner sails on her maiden voyage. She is dressed overall, the band plays, the sirens sound, the streamers are thrown, and the crowds cheer, but her Master and crew know that this is not a normal, but a special occasion. Thereafter she will sail and dock with little excitement. How thrilling it is to read, in the early chapters of the Acts, of the wonderful things that happened when the Holy Spirit was first given and the New Testament Church was born. Three thousand people are converted through one sermon, whilst miracles and signs are commonplace, but in spite of the fact that some would have us believe otherwise, those were not ordinary days. As Luke unfolds the story of the early Church, he makes it clear that miracles were not so easily wrought, or souls so easily won. Luke begins his story in the city of Jerusalem (chapter 1), and concludes in the city of Rome (chapter 28). Peter, full of the Holy Ghost, began his ministry in extraordinary days, while Paul, also full of the Holy Ghost and faith, concluded his ministry in more normal times, and Luke concludes his record by giving us one final picture of the apostles in action, and the 20th century Church would do well to consider carefully its significance:

> And so we went toward Rome. And from thence, when the brethren heard of us, they came to meet us as far as Appii forum, and the three taverns: whom when Paul saw, he thanked God, and took courage. And when we came to Rome, the centurion delivered the prisoners to the captain of the guard: but Paul was suffered *to dwell by himself* with a soldier that kept him. And it came to pass, that after three days Paul called the chief of the Jews together, and . . . *there came many to him into his lodging*; to whom he expounded and testified the kingdom of God, persuading them concerning Jesus, both out of the law of Moses, and out of the prophets, from morning till evening. And some believed the things which were spoken, and some believed not. And when they agreed not among themselves (Paul

said) Be it known therefore unto you, that the salvation of God is sent unto the Gentiles, and that they will hear it. And when he had said these words, the Jews departed, and had great reasoning among themselves. *And Paul dwelt two whole years in his own hired house,* and received all that came in unto him, preaching the kingdom of God, and teaching those things which concern the Lord Jesus Christ, with all confidence, no man forbidding him. – Acts 28: 14–17; 23–25; 28–31.

Yes, the aged Apostle is still using the same technique: eighteen months of home-based evangelism in Corinth, three years in Ephesus, and now two whole years in his own hired house in Rome. How I wish I could have been amongst his guests listening week after week, month after month throughout those two years whilst Paul was leading that Bible Cell in his Roman home, expounding, testifying, and persuading concerning Jesus out of the law and the prophets from morning till evening; with burning love and warm-hearted hospitality, preaching and teaching Jesus Christ! Magnificent cathedrals and costly churches may or may not have been built by the apostles, but one thing is beyond question, for the most part, the New Testament Church met in one another's homes for prayer, fellowship, Bible Study, and evangelism.

Yes, there is no escape – *this* was the apostolic method of evangelism, and *this* should be our method too! There's no short cut; no easy way; no escaping our responsibilities or salving our consciences by supporting professional evangelists to do for us what we ourselves are not prepared to do. *We* must get deeply involved with our workmates and neighbours in praying for them by name, in opening our hearts and homes to them, in getting to know them, in showing them practical Christian kindness and love, and working patiently and tirelessly towards their conversion.

ROMAN CATHOLICS TOO

Yes, everywhere in Britain, on the American continent, and throughout the world you'll find these groups in operation, and every day new ones springing up spontaneously, and often in the most unlikely places. For instance, Roman Catholic laymen in Britain are being encouraged to gather in their homes to read and study the Revised Standard Version of the Bible, without priest or commentary – this to my mind is intensely exciting, and highly explosive too!

I went into the Catholic Truth Society's Westminster Bookshop recently to buy a Catholic edition of the R.S.V. for a devout Catholic woman who had just turned to Christ at one of our conferences, and whilst I was being served I asked the head saleswoman:

"Do you sell many copies of this edition of the Bible?"

"Sell many?" she replied, "We sell them by the hundred!"

The great Catholic Bookshop in O'Connell Street, Dublin, was devoting one of their large display windows exclusively to the Catholic R.S.V. edition (almost identical to the Protestant edition). I went in and talked to the salesman.

"How are the R.S.V. versions selling here in Ireland?"

"Selling them?" he said, "we can hardly keep pace with the sales. What is more that version of the Bible is now on the School Curriculum throughout the Republic of Eire, and every school-child without exception has his own copy."

I heard the same story when I visited the vast Catholic Bookshop near the Pennsylvania station in New York City.

During my last visit to the States I was invited to lead a Bible Cell Study Group in a home on the Eastern seaboard. More than thirty people turned out that night. Sitting just inside the door, dressed in slacks was a man in his mid-forties who took part three or four times during the study, bringing out most helpful comments. During coffee, which was served at the end of the meeting, this man came over and talked to me.

"I want to thank you for that study tonight. I found it most helpful. This is the third Home Bible Study Meeting that I have attended in the past few months. I must say I love them. Incidentally I am the Roman Catholic Priest in charge of the church just up the street."

If a small seed germinates under a slab of concrete, it will split it! When men and women – Catholic or Protestant, Nonconformist or Anglican, religious or irreligious, take the Holy Bible in their hands, and expose themselves to its message, miracles are bound to happen – and what is more – they *are* happening! Be of good cheer!

Don't imagine that the devil is not making full use of this widespread demand for Home Bible Study Groups, believe me, every cranky movement is making capital out of it! That dangerous American cult who call themselves 'Jehovah's Witnesses' have started hundreds of groups, and taken over others to propagate their Unitarian heresies, and disrupt the Christian Church. If Bible-loving ministers and Christian people do not step in immediately and exploit this situation for the furtherance of New

Testament truth – then, make no mistake, the enemy will do so for his own ends!

Recently I have been asking myself this question again and again. 'Is the 20th-century Church being driven back from a vast man-made organisation to the vital Spirit-inspired organism of the first century Church?'

Variety—The Spice of Life

THERE is nothing quite so stimulating to our spiritual life as hearing what God is doing elsewhere for, and through, our fellow Christians. In the Revival of 1859 in Northern Ireland the work spread across the Province through people moving from place to place telling of what God was doing. And I am writing this book to tell from my own experience what God is doing today, so that the hearts of my fellow Christians might be warmed and stirred to become personally involved in this movement of the Spirit.

Our God is the God of infinite variety; each blade of grass differs from every other; no two experiences of conversion are alike, and one of the many indications that the Bible Cells are of God is the infinite variety there is amongst them. Each one is unique, and has its own emphasis. There is no sign of mass production; each bears the stamp of the Master Craftsman, that hall-mark of divine originality. One concentrates mainly on Bible Study, another on Prayer and yet another on Evangelistic Outreach. Some are strictly Church-based, others are interdenominational, whilst others are entirely independent. This one is led by a minister, that one by a dedicated business man, this by a young Christian couple, and that has no leader at all! Sometimes two or more Cells work in close harmony, from time to time meeting up together, whilst others are completely isolated. I have come across many who had no idea that other Cells existed. Some Cells meet at breakfast time, some mid-morning, some in the afternoon, and many others in the evening. Some meet only once a month, others alternate weeks, but the majority find that once a week is ideal. An hotel lounge or café is the venue for some; for others it's the manse; for a few, a very few, it is the church hall or vestry, but the majority meet in private homes. Some always meet in the same home; others alternate between two, whilst others deliberately move 'from house to house'! This Cell meets only in Christian homes, whilst that one, for strategic reasons, seeks hospitality in the non-Christian household, and yet another uses sympathetic homes for Bible Study and Prayer, and non-Christian homes for Guest Nights. Some Cells start with refreshments; others say 'goodbye' over a cup of coffee, whilst many have no refreshments at all! Although redeemed people always love singing, the majority of Bible Cells devote all their time to Bible Study and Prayer, leaving the singing of Psalms and hymns to services for public worship and exhortation. There are no rules. "Where the Spirit of the Lord is there is liberty!"

Because the Bible Cells are so obviously the strategic operation of God's Spirit to meet the needs of this hour, I have in the last three or four years spent much of my time travelling many thousands of miles in Britain and on the American continent visiting countless Cells, watching, listening, asking questions, trying to discern what God is doing, and how He is doing it. Moreover, I have organised and led a number of both residential and day conferences for members and leaders of Bible Cells. I don't pretend to be an expert in this field, or to know all the answers, but over the months I have seen that although each Cell is unique, there are five significant characteristics common to all. Having named them, I should like to say something about each, which will, I hope, prove useful both to those who are already involved, and those who are prayerfully considering forming new Cells. Here, then, are the five common characteristics. There is no significance in the order in which they are set out.

FIVE COMMON CHARACTERISTICS

1. BIBLE STUDY: Every Cell that I have visited regards the Bible as the final authority for faith and conduct, and devotes much time to a prayerful reading and study of the Word.

2. PRAYER: Every Bible Cell gives priority to the ministry of prayer, both private and corporate. Whilst thanksgiving, confession, and worship are seldom overlooked, intercession undoubtedly takes priority, especially for the spiritual needs of non-Christian individuals and families in the community.

3. FELLOWSHIP: One of the main objects of every Cell is that the members may help and encourage one another in spiritual development, and in effective Christian witness.

4. EVANGELISM: Whereas in the first place many Bible Cells were formed for the purpose of helping one another through Bible Study, prayer, and fellowship, members invariably develop a deep desire to see their non-Christian relatives and neighbours turn to Christ. Where this does not happen, the Cell often withers and dies.

5. GOOD WORKS: Throughout the world, Bible Cells have this in common: they have a deep and intensely practical love both for one another and their neighbours. This love manifests itself not only in praying and witnessing, but also in practical works of kindness and mercy.

It is perhaps unnecessary to point out that these five characteristics are also found in the New Testament Church. The balance between the characteristics varies a good deal from Cell to Cell. Some devote most of their time to the study of Scripture, leaving comparatively little for prayer; some concentrate largely on prayer, and others on evangelism, and so on, but – and this is very important – the healthiest and most effective Cells are beyond doubt those which maintain an even balance between Bible, prayer, fellowship, evangelism, and good works.

And now, let's look in on various Bible Cells, and see them at work, and to help us think clearly, we will examine the various activities in the order in which they are set out above. The first of the five common characteristics of Bible Cells is their emphasis on the reading and study of the Bible.

I. BIBLE STUDY

A considerable number of Cells were started with the express purpose of studying the Scriptures, and were therefore given such descriptions which many still hold, such as 'Bible Study Circle', 'Home Bible Group', 'Mr. Jacob's Bible Study', 'Bible Coffee Morning', etc., and although some Cells do not major on the study of Scripture, I have not come across one at which the Bible is not at least read regularly. The Cells in which Bible Study does not play an active part are very much in the minority. The various methods of study used in the Cells are far too numerous to describe here, but it may prove useful if we take a look at some of them.

VERSE-BY-VERSE

One of the most common, and to my mind by far the best method, is the verse-by-verse Bible Study. We have already 'sat in' with the Warren Farm Bible Cell, as they used this method in their study of Naaman the leper, but may I urge you to go back once again to Warren Farm, take a Bible, notebook and pencil with you, and tell Mr. Thornton you have come as a student to watch, listen, learn, and make notes as to exactly how he leads the Study. Observe his tact, consideration, and method. Be sure to write down the answers to the following questions: How did the Group get their Bibles? What did they do before they started the Study? In what ways did Mr. Thornton show consideration for the people? How did they read the chapter? What sort of chapter background information did the Leader give? What sort of questions did Mr. Thornton ask before the chapter was read? Immediately following the reading, the leader gave some good advice on how to meditate. What was this advice? What good Bible Commentary did he recommend? (Be sure you get full details, your own Cell will find them *most* helpful!) Finally, copy out fully those excellent questions printed on the Cards they use at Warren Farm as an aid to meditation. Write them down fully, and then memorise them – off you go now, back to page 20.

off you go now, back to page 20.

THE TEENAGERS' CELL

Now I want you to come with me to another part of the country to visit a Teenagers' Bible Cell. This Cell, like many another, is very democratic; they have no official leader, although you will soon recognise two or three natural leaders amongst them. The members consist mainly of senior schoolboys and girls who meet after school once a week in the home of a sixth former, near the centre of the town. The average attendance is about twenty-two (I think it would be better if they divided into two groups). They only have buns and lemonade on special occasions, and like all healthy Cells, they ring the changes on the type of meetings they have. Sometimes one of their number just 'gives a brief thought' and they spend the rest of the time in prayer; other times they have an open evangelistic meeting, when they invite a guest speaker, and so on; but today they are having a verse by verse Bible Study, not the first one by any means, so they are all well acquainted with this method of study. Let's go!

Sorry about the noise, they'll soon settle down! Oh yes, here's Vivian who has been appointed as this afternoon's leader. "Vivian – meet my friend, Mr. Reader, who has come as an observer – he's thinking of starting a Bible Cell too. Mr. Reader, Vivian is a school prefect, and comes from a good Christian home, her parents are close friends of ours."

Those who are able to find a chair are fortunate, the rest must sit on the floor. The hubbub is dying down now, and one of the boys says:

"Next week we're having a 'loaves and fishes' meeting; that is, we shall share with one another any good thoughts we have had in our own Bible Reading during the week, so look out for good titbits, we don't want to sit here in silence for an hour – it's up to you! Also we shall have a fifteen-minute chain verse competition. Someone will start by quoting their favourite verse, then someone else will think of a parallel verse that has an obvious connection with the first, and quote that, then if we can, we'll find the reference too, and so on. This will be a good mental and spiritual exercise for us all. Now this afternoon we are having a verse by verse, and Vivian West is choosing the passage and leading the study. Over to you Vivian."

Vivian is now sitting on the arm of an easy chair in the corner.

"Thank you, Maurice," says Vivian. "Before we start, if you don't already have one of the meditation question cards, please put your hand up, and I'll pass you one." Several hands go up, including mine. The cards are identical to those used at Warren Farm.

"Now I want to ask you to put all you can into the study, not for your own sake, but for ours. I'm sure we shall have a good time. The passage I have chosen is Luke chapter 5, verses 1 to 11."

And as we all find the place, Vivian continues:

"Tonight, instead of asking someone to lead in prayer, we are going to have silent prayer, and I want you each to pray, first for yourself, then others in the group, and then for me. Ask that God will speak to each of us, and that we may not only be hearers, but also doers of His Word. Let us pray."

It is a moving sight to see a company of young people like this sitting with their heads bowed in prayer and their Bibles open in front of them – take courage; this is happening everywhere! I believe that God, through these Bible Cells is preparing this generation for a situation and trials that their parents know nothing of.

Vivian says "Amen" out loud, and we all look up.

"I'll try to keep my introduction short," she says, "or there may be complaints! This passage that we are going to study is not the story of Peter's conversion – you'll find that in John chapter 1. This is the story of how Peter, his brother Andrew, and their partners James and John, all of whom were already the disciples (students) of Jesus, were called by Him to leave their fishing and follow Him as His apostles (special messengers). The key verse is the verse 10 – 'Fear not; from henceforth thou shalt catch men.' Up to this time they were only interested in catching fish; from now on they are going to catch men – in the Gospel net. And we have got to do the same. This story is full of good ideas for fishers, and teaches us what to do (and what not to do) in trying to capture others for Christ. I have one or two other things I want to say after our reading, but first, one or two pronunciations which might worry some of you. 'Gennesaret' is pronounced as it is spelt with a hard 'G' as in 'gun'. The word 'draught' in verses 4 and 9 refers to the fish which were enclosed in the net, and rhymes with 'draft' not 'taught'! There are no other difficult words, so let's read the 11 verses out loud slowly in unison. And to save confusion, those of you who are *not* using the Authorised (King James') Version, please keep quiet!"

FISHERS OF MEN

1 And it came to pass, that, as the people pressed upon him to hear the word of God, he stood by the lake of Gennesaret. *2* And saw two ships standing by the lake: but the fishermen were gone out of them, and were washing their nets. *3* And he entered into one of the ships, which was Simon's, and prayed him that he would thrust out a little from the land. And he sat down, and taught the people out of the ship. *4* Now when he had left speaking, he said unto Simon, Launch out into the deep, and let down your nets for a draught. *5* And Simon answering said unto him, Master, we have toiled all the night, and have taken nothing: nevertheless at thy word I will let down the net. *6* And when they had this done, they inclosed a great multitude of fishes: and their net brake. *7* And they beckoned unto their partners, which were in the other ship, that they should come and help them. And they came, and filled both the ships, so that they began to sink. *8* When Simon Peter saw it, he fell down at Jesus' knees, saying, Depart from me; for I am a sinful man, O Lord. *9* For he was astonished, and all that were with him, at the draught of the fishes which they had taken: *10* And so was also James, and John, the sons of Zebedee, which were partners with Simon. And Jesus said unto Simon, Fear not; from henceforth thou shalt catch men. *11* And when they had brought their ships to land, they forsook all, and followed him. – Luke 5: 1–11.

"Now before we start," says Vivian, "verse 1 – Lake Gennesaret – this is the same lake which elsewhere is called 'the Lake of Tiberias' and 'the Sea of Galilee'. Gennesaret was a lakeside town. Verse 2 – 'fishermen . . . washing their nets' – this happened in the early morning. The best time to catch fish on this lake is at night. Verse 3 – 'He taught the people'. What He taught them is recorded in Matthew 13. This miracle should not be confused with a similar one which Jesus performed after His resurrection; that's in John chapter 21. And now we're ready to go. Let's take verse 1 by itself. Jack, will you please read it to us, and then we'll have one minute for silent prayer and meditation before we share our thoughts."

Jack reads the first verse. In the silence we all pray and ask ourselves the questions set out on our Bible Meditation Cards.

"Right," said the prefect, "now, if you've got anything you can share with us, a thought ... a parallel verse, a question, anything ... put your hand up, and I'll give you a number."

It's a bit sticky at first, but now a hand goes up.

"Thank you, you will be no. 1," then another, "no. 2," which is quickly followed by no. 3.

"Now," says Vivian, "that will do for a start, and we'll have your thoughts please in that order."

I like this idea, don't you? It gets the nasty silences over all at once!

A delightful boy with a freckled face, red curly hair and a snub nose is no. 1: "The people pressed upon Him to hear the Word of God," he says, "and I can see a good example here for me – I ought to be keen on hearing God's Word like they were."

Now no. 2 speaks up:

"There must have been a very big crowd of people, and those right at the back might have found it very difficult, or even impossible, to hear the Word of God. It was those who were nearest to Jesus who heard best, and I find that the nearer I live to Jesus, the plainer do I hear the Word of God·in the Bible. Sometimes I get so far away I can't hear anything – the Bible seems quite dry."

No. 3 is a tall, dark girl of fifteen or sixteen who obviously has been brought up on a daily diet of the Bible!

"I wondered why it was that the common people were always so keen to hear Jesus, why it was that they 'pressed upon him to hear the Word of God', and I have found two verses which answer my question. The first is in Luke 4 verse 32, 'And they were astonished at his doctrine: for his Word was with power', and the other is in Luke 5 verse 17, 'And it came to pass on a certain day, as he was teaching . . . the power of the Lord was present to heal them.' I think people crowded round Jesus because 'His Word was with power' and 'the power of the Lord was present'. I think too that the secret of this power, this authority in the preaching of Jesus is found here in chapter 5:16. 'He withdrew himself into the wilderness, and prayed.' And through this God has reminded me that if my witness is to be effective, I too must get alone with God and pray."

Here the Leader speaks up again.

"Thank you – those were really good thoughts. Let's have some more like them, and don't be afraid if, after you have been given a number, someone else steals your thought before it's your turn to speak. You can always say, "my thought has already been expressed."

"Now, I think we'll take verses 2 and 3 together. Anne, will you please read the verses for us?" (My guess is that Vivian is purposely choosing folk to read who will benefit from hearing their own voices in public.)

CLEAN NETS

Anne's reading is followed again by one minute of silence, broken only by the turning of the sacred page. Then five new hands go up, and each person is given a number, and once again we're off.

"The fishermen were washing their nets – you can't catch fish with dirty nets, and this reminds me that my life must be clean. I must be consistent if I'm to win others for Christ."

At this point someone else butts in.

"There's a verse somewhere about our being clean vessels if God is to use us, I think it's somewhere in Timothy."

There's a hectic turning of leaves as Vivian says:

"The first person to find it please read it out."

Two folk start almost together. "I've got it! It's in 2 Timothy 2: 20, 21.

"But in a great house there are not only vessels of gold and of silver, but also of wood and of earth; and some to honour, and some to dishonour. If a man therefore purge himself from these, he shall be a vessel unto honour, sanctified, and meet for the Master's use, and prepared unto every good work."

"My thought is based on verse 3: 'He entered into Simon's ship . . . sat down, and taught the people out of the ship.' I don't expect Peter's boat was any bigger or better than any other, but it was there at hand and available to Jesus, so He used it. I think that my life and my gifts should be ready for Christ too, and if I ask Him in, and give Him all I've got, perhaps He'll come in and teach other people through me."

"My thought was rather like the last one," says another. "The Lord wants to use my life as a base from which He can teach and win others. I also thought that just as Peter had to 'thrust out a little from the land' before his boat could be used, perhaps we too should see that our lives are separate from the world if He is going to use us. I hope that's not too far fetched!"

The last speaker on verses 2 and 3 says:

"Jesus was always teaching people the Word of God. I can see an example here that I should follow. Many people know little or nothing of the Bible or the Gospel. I must try to teach them the truth."

"Let's take verses 4, 5 and 6 together," says Vivian, "And we're glad to have Mary Johnson with us tonight for the first time, so Mary will you please read the verses to us, then after the meditation I'm going to reserve this section for folk who haven't spoken yet – so you others will have to pipe down."

IN SEASON – OUT OF SEASON

After Mary's reading and the silence, four new hands go up.

No. 1 says: "I have found a parallel on verse 5, 'Master, we have toiled all the night . . . nevertheless at Thy Word' – in fact it was the text our minister preached on last Sunday morning: 'Preach the Word; be instant in season, out of season; reprove, rebuke, exhort with all longsuffering and doctrine' " (2 Tim. 4: 2).

No. 2: "The Lord's command to Peter 'Launch out into the deep, and let down your nets for a draught' – I think this is an exciting command – we must not hug the shore and play for safety. We must get out into the deep and dangerous water where the fish are, if we are going to catch them. I wonder if William Carey was thinking of this verse when he said, 'Attempt great things for God and expect great things from God'? "

No. 3: "I can see how easy it is for us to get into a rut in our Christian work – 'Master, we have toiled all the night . . . nevertheless at Thy Word.' Sometimes we go on doing things in the same way because they have always been done like that. God's Word is more important than our customs and traditions. There's a verse – I don't know where it is, where Jesus says: 'You make God's Word of no effect by your traditions.' We must keep in touch with the Lord, and do what He says, just when He tells us to do it."

It takes a few minutes for us to find the parallel verse quoted by No. 3, but someone unearths it in Matthew chapter 15, verse 6, "Ye made the commandment of God of none effect by your tradition."

No. 4: "In verse 4 Jesus told Peter 'Let down your nets' (plural), but Peter replied, 'Nevertheless at Thy Word I will let down the net' (singular), and because of this 'their net brake' and many fishes escaped. God reminded me that I must guard against unbelief and disobedience."

"Can anyone," says Vivian, "think of a verse that sums up that thought?"

There's quite a long pause before someone says:

"According to your faith be it unto you," but we search in vain for the reference.

No. 5: "I've found a verse here in Matthew 4: 21 which is a parallel verse on verse 6 'and their net brake'. It says that James and John were in a ship mending their nets when Jesus called them. We need a spiritual overhaul sometimes if we are going to catch men for the Lord."

Vivian says, "We will take verses 7 and 8 together, but instead of asking someone to read them aloud this time, we will read them silently."

And now three hands go up.

No. 1: " 'And they came, and filled both the ships, so that they began to sink.' I've found a parallel verse in the Old Testament. I think it's one of my favourite texts – Malachi 3: 10: 'Bring ye all the tithes into the storehouse, that there may be meat in mine house, and prove me now herewith, saith the Lord of hosts, if I will not open you the windows of heaven, and pour you out a blessing, that there shall not be room enough to receive it.' When we give God our best, He gives us back much more."

No. 2: "Verse 7, 'And they beckoned unto their partners, which were in the other ship, that they should come and help them. And they came.' God has reminded me through this verse that if we are to be successful in winning others for Christ, we must work together with other Christians as partners. We must be ready to help others, and ask them to help us."

Vivian: "Yes, there's a good example of Peter and John working and praying together in partnership in Acts chapter 3: 'Now Peter and John went up together into the temple at the hour of prayer. . . .' And now no. 3."

No. 3: "Well, . . . I've got a question I should like to ask. Why did Peter kneel down and ask Jesus to leave him, as it says in verse 8?"

"Can anyone help Anthony on this?" asks Vivian.

One of the boys suggests that perhaps Peter was ashamed of himself because he only let down one net, when Jesus had told him to let down all the nets.

"No," says one of the girls, "I don't think that was the reason. I think it was because, through the miracle, Peter recognised that Jesus was the Son of God, and this made him feel how sinful he was, and how holy Jesus was, and so he knelt down and worshipped Jesus."

Another boy: "Yes, I agree with Sandra. Isaiah felt like Peter when he had a vision of God, and he said: 'Woe is me for I am undone.' "

Vivian: "I am sorry, but I'm afraid we'll have to stop here – not only the discussion, but also the verse-by-verse study. We must save the last ten minutes for prayer. If you want to go on into verse 9 to 11, you can do it when you get home. Now, before we have prayer for other people, we are going to have a number of short prayers based on this passage we have been studying – not long prayers, just a sentence each."

This is interesting.

"O Lord Jesus Christ, help us, like Peter, to realise how sinful we are, and how wonderful You are, and help us to worship You – Amen."

"O Lord, save us from being shallow-water Christians. Help us to launch out into the deep and be fishers of men – Amen."

"We thank Thee, Lord, for the Bible. Help us to press upon You and live near to You every day that we, like these people, may hear the Word of God – Amen."

"Please help us, Lord, like James and John, to be ready to go and help other Christians in their work for Thee – Amen."

"According to your faith, be it unto you. Save us, O Lord, from unbelief. Give us a strong faith in You. Help us to do immediately what You tell us to do, and do it with all our might – Amen."

"O God, save us from getting into a rut. May we never do anything, pray, read the Bible, or work for Thee just out of habit. May we be guided by Thee in everything – Amen."

"Lord Jesus, we thank You for teaching the people out of Peter's boat. Help us to give our lives to You, so that You can enter in and teach and bless others through us – Amen."

"We have been reminded Lord that You do not call lazy but industrious people into Your service. As Peter and his partners were busy washing and mending their nets, help us to follow their example, and do our daily work well for Thee, in class, at home, and on the playing field – Amen."

And now, I am sorry to butt in dear Mr. Reader, but we just haven't got time to stay for the general prayer session.

Yes, I thought you would be surprised! I have attended scores of verse-by-verse studies over the past few years for groups of varying ages, and I find that the best ones are invariably those for teenagers.

The 'Subject' Method

ANOTHER method of study frequently used in Bible Cells is that of the 'subject' method. A Biblical theme is selected such as the Trinity, the Deity of Christ, the Nature of Man, Sin, Redemption, Temptation, or Prayer, and then, aided by a Concordance, and a Chain Reference Bible, texts of Scripture dealing with the subject are studied. This is a method much favoured by Bible Cells in the U.S.A., and from time to time can make a useful change from the verse-by-verse method.

Before we visit a Bible Cell in action on one of these subject studies, I should like to point out two dangers which, in this form of study, should be carefully watched.

First, almost *anything* can be proved by using isolated proof texts. For instance, you can show that the atheist is right simply by quoting Psalm 14: 1 'There is no God', but this same text taken in its context makes very different reading: 'The fool hath said in his heart, there is no God. . . .' Remember, that as the one phrase in this example can be misunderstood when taken out of its setting, so also are many whole verses when not considered in the light of the chapters or the book in which they were written. Scripture must always be interpreted in the light of Scripture. I once heard Dr. Campbell Morgan say: "A text without a context is a pretext."

The majority of religious cults and heresies spring from this dangerous practice of studying the Bible by proof texts. Jehovah's Witnesses are often credited, quite wrongly with being great Bible students, whereas in fact they have simply mastered a number of proof texts, many of which are taken out of their context, and with these they 'disprove' the Trinity and Deity of our Lord Jesus Christ, and other great Biblical doctrines.

A man once told me that he knew virtually all there was to know about the subject of Justification, for he said, "I have memorised every text in which the words 'justify' and 'justification' appear". In course of conversation I found he really knew very little of the subject. If a man really wants to understand Justification, he must first master the entire Roman and Galatian Epistles.

The second danger to be watched in this 'subject' method of

study is that of the Cell becoming lopsided in its doctrinal emphasis. The leaders, or the entire Cell, may easily major on some pet theme such as Prophecy, Divine Healing, Tongues, Predestination, British Israelism, Revival, Prayer, Pacifism, Baptism, Christian Politics, Sex, the Second Blessing, or what have you, whilst other great Biblical themes will be inevitably overlooked.

MARION LAWSON'S CELL

Now having issued my warnings, let's do another 'sit in'. This time it's a Women's Coffee Morning in a small town in Upper New York State. The moving light behind this Bible Cell is Marion Lawson, a doctor's wife.

The Cell meets each Thursday morning in the large and comfortable home of Martha Amhurst at about 10.15, and each member as she arrives helps herself to a cup of coffee and a cookie, which is by interpretation a biscuit. The average attendance is fourteen. At 10.40 Martha puts the coffee pot and cookies away – those who arrive after this miss the refreshments – for at 10.45 precisely the study begins. (It closes just as promptly at 11.45.) Most of the women in this Cell are members of a good Bible-based community Church in the area, and are therefore fairly well instructed.

Like every other 'live' Cell they ring the changes on the type of meetings they have. Last week, apart from a short reading and exhortation from one of their number, they spent the entire hour in prayer. Today, however, they are doing a 'subject' Bible Study on the theme of 'Love'. Last Thursday, in preparation for today's study, each woman was given a question on the subject, and since there were only four basic questions, this means that three or four women had the same question, and during the week they have been praying and searching the Bible for their answers.

When the Cell was first formed Marion, who has always been responsible for planning the studies, prepared fourteen different questions on the subject to be studied – one for each member, but this did not work out too well because (i) some folk were unable to attend and therefore key questions were left unanswered; (ii) some of the members, either through slackness or mental inability, came up with answers which were right off the beam, and (iii) it was found that fourteen questions were far too many to discuss in one session.

"I find it far better," Marion told me, "to prepare four really provocative questions which will encourage folk to pray and study their Bibles. After all, our main object is to stimulate further private study."

Well, here we are, help yourself to some coffee and a cookie. (I love American coffee, don't you, but avoid their tea like the plague. There's only one thing worse, and that's English coffee!) Oh yes, here's our leader. "Marion, meet my friend, Mr. Reader, who is planning to start a Bible Cell in his own home. It's kind of you to let us come in as observers. We promise that being mere males we will keep quiet!"

Let's sit over here where we can see, but not be seen. We only just got our coffee in time. . . it's nearly time to start.

A GUEST LUNCHEON

Taking her cue from Marion, a woman says:

"Now folk, it's time we were off, please be seated, it's my turn this week to make the announcements. Next week as you all know is our special Guest Luncheon, and instead of meeting here, we shall be having a lunch at 12.30 in the Dixie Room at Louis Cherry's Restaurant in the central shopping plaza. This is an outreach effort to introduce our non-Christian neighbours to the Gospel. Our guest speaker is Heather Olford of New York City, whose husband is Dr. Stephen Olford, pastor of a big city church. Heather has a great testimony to give, which she gives with a delightful Irish accent. As a bait to attract the non-Christian women she is speaking on 'Bringing up a Christian family in New York City' – the Olfords live right on West 57th Street, near Central Park, so she knows what she's talking about! We shall have a light lunch, and then Gloria Putnum, our pastor's wife, will introduce the speaker, and she will go right ahead, and if there's time we'll have some questions too. So, if you have a neighbour who is having problems with her teenage young people, here's your chance! Now the lunch is only $2.50 a plate, but in order to come, you must have not only a ticket, but also a neighbour – preferably a non-Christian – as your guest. We have promised Heather Olford that more than half the number will be non-Christian women. Jane tells me that nearly sixty tickets have gone already, so work as if it all depended on you, and pray as if it all depended on the Lord, and we shall have a grand time. Remember, this Bible Cell is run not just for ourselves, but also for non-members. When we cease to help others we had better go out of business!

"Now today we are having a Bible Study on the subject of 'Love', and here is Marion who has planned the study to lead us. . . ."

57

"Before I introduce this morning's subject," says Marion, "I have asked Lois Schneider to lead us in a prayer, asking for the guidance of the Holy Spirit."

Lois prays. . . .

A GOOD INTRODUCTION

Marion's introduction is both informative and stimulating.

"We have chosen one of the greatest Bible themes there is – 'The Love of God'. Paul says, 'it passeth knowledge' – Ephesians 3: 19. We have often heard George Beverly Shea singing on the radio:

"Could we with ink the ocean fill,
And were the skies of parchment made;
Were every stalk on earth a quill,
And every man a scribe by trade;
To write the love of God above
Would drain the ocean dry;
Nor could the scroll contain the whole,
Tho' stretched from sky to sky.

so you see it's unlikely we shall exhaust the subject in the next fifty-five minutes! However, we shall try to say something about 'the Love of God' – His love for His Son, His people, and a lost world, and we will discuss our love for God, for our fellow Christians, and for the lost.

"When last week I announced today's subject, you may remember Clare Aitkinson said: 'Now that's a good subject – Love – I just *can't* love my enemies; in fact there are some of my relatives I don't even like, so heaven help my enemies!' We smile, but don't we all feel the same? So to help us think clearly, let me tell you first what Christian love really is.

"The Greek language, in which the New Testament was originally written, has at least four distinct words for love, each of which we translate either as 'love' or 'charity'.

"First, there is the word *eros* (the verb is *eran*) which is the desire that one sex has for another. I think it is a pity we use the word 'love' in this connection, for there is so much in our modern world which is called 'love' which is really little more than base greed and lust. This word *eros* is not found in the New Testament.

"Second, there is the word *philia* (the verb is *philein*). This is the word used by John in his Gospel where he tells us that Jesus *loved* Lazarus, Martha and Mary, chapter 11 verses 5 and 36. It is used to describe genuine affection between friends.

58

Storgē – Family affection

"Third, there is the word *storgē* which is mainly to do with family affection, love between parents and children. Neither the noun *storgē* nor the verb *stergein* are found in the New Testament, but the related adjective *philostorgos* is used by Paul in the tenth verse of that very practical chapter 12 of Romans, and the King James' Version translates the word 'kindly affectioned'. 'Let love be without dissimulation. Abhor that which is evil; cleave to that which is good. Be *kindly affectioned* one to another with brotherly love.'

"Fourthly, the great New Testament word for Christian love is *agapē* (the verb is *agapan*). 'God is Love' (*agapē*). 'If God so loved (*agapan*) us, we ought also to love (*agapan*) one another.'

"Whilst *eros* (passion), *philia* (warm affection) and *storgē* (family affection) are all to do with human emotion, the Christian *agapē* (love) is not so much a matter of emotion, but rather an attitude of mind, a principle which governs our thoughts, words, and actions. It is deeply involved with the human will.

"In His Sermon on the Mount Jesus said, 'I say unto you love (*agapan*) your enemies.' He did not tell us to feel sentimental about them, as a boys feels about his girl friend (*eran*), or as we feel about our children (*stergein*), nor did He tell us to *like* them. No, He said Love (*agapan*) them. That is, we are to adopt and maintain a certain attitude of mind and will toward them which refuses to say or do anything which will cause them pain. And in the same passage He gave concrete examples of what love (*agapē*) really is, and how it reacts and behaves toward those who are vicious, covetous, domineering, selfish, hateful, and unjust. Before we start our discussion, I am going to ask Maralyn Olsen to read that passage to us. It is found in Matthew 5 verses 38 to 48."

Love your enemies

"You have heard that it was said, 'An eye for an eye and a tooth for a tooth.' But I say to you, Do not resist one who is evil. But if any one strikes you on the right cheek, turn to him the other also; and if any one would sue you and take your coat, let him have your cloak as well; and if any one forces you to go one mile, go with him two miles. Give to him who begs from you, and do not refuse him who would borrow from you. You have heard that it was said, 'You shall love your neighbour and hate your enemy.' But I say to you, Love your enemies and pray for those who persecute you, so that you may be sons of your Father who is in heaven; for he makes his sun rise on the evil and on the good, and sends rain on the just and on the unjust. For if you love those who love you, what reward have you? Do not even the tax collectors do the same? And if you salute only your brethren, what more are you doing than others? Do not even the Gentiles do the same? You, therefore, must be perfect, as your heavenly Father is perfect."

THE FIRST QUESTION

"Thank you, Maralyn," says Marion. "Now, last week I gave each of you a card bearing your name and a question. Each question is numbered. We have a total of four different questions, and each question has been given to three members of the Cell for their consideration. We shall take the questions in the order in which they are numbered. I shall call on one of the three women who have the first question to read it out and give her findings, then we shall ask the other two if they have anything to add, then we shall have a brief, general discussion, and then on to the second question, and so on. Now let's start with question number one. According to my list here, this question was given to Clare Aitkinson, Henrietta Sandman, and Marlise Hoffman. Marlise, will you please read question no. 1, and lead off."

Marlise has opened her Bible and taken from it her question card and some notes she has made. She reads the first question: "According to the Bible, how important is Love?" Now she unfolds her notes and continues. . . . "It seems to me that love is one of the most important things in all the world. The Lord says that the first and greatest commandment is that we give Him ALL our love, and the second commandment is that we love others as much as we love ourselves. I have found it here in Matthew chapter 22 verses 37-40:

" 'Jesus said unto him, Thou shalt love the Lord thy God with all thy heart, and with all thy soul, and with all thy mind. This is the first and great commandment. And the second is like unto it, Thou shalt love thy neighbour as thyself. On these two commandments hang all the law and the prophets.'

"Here Jesus tells us that love is 'first' and love is 'great', also that every other commandment is based on these two commands to love. I also found a parallel passage in Romans 13, verses 8 through 10:

" 'Owe no man any thing, but to love one another: for he that loveth another hath fulfilled the law. For this, Thou shalt not commit adultery, Thou shalt not kill, Thou shalt not steal, Thou shalt not bear false witness, Thou shalt not covet; and if there be any other commandment, it is briefly comprehended in this saying, namely, Thou shalt love thy neighbour as thyself. Love worketh no ill to his neighbour: therefore love is the fulfilling of the law.'

"Now, until I started to look this up last week I always thought that faith was the most important thing of all, but I have come across a verse here which puts me right on this – it's 1 Corinthians 13: 13 – this double 13 is certainly an unlucky number to my false notion – it is not FAITH, but LOVE which is the greatest:

" 'And now abideth faith, hope, charity, these three; but the greatest of these is charity.'

"I had one other thought I'd like to share with the group, and it's this. The thing God values most highly is our love. This is clear from the first and great commandment. I think the opposite of love is not hate but indifference, and the thing God hates most is our indifference, or lack of love. This is clear from Revelation chapter 2: 4, 5 and 3: 15, 16.

" 'Nevertheless I have somewhat against thee, because thou hast left thy first love. Remember therefore from whence thou art fallen, and repent, and do the first works; . . . I know thy works, that thou art neither cold nor hot: I would thou wert cold or hot. So then because thou art lukewarm, and neither cold nor hot, I will spue thee out of my mouth.' "

(Mr. Reader, make a note of how, whenever a scripture reference is given, the speaker waits for the group to find the verses in their own Bibles before reading, and see also how each member jots down the references in her notebook. Make sure your group does likewise!)

THOUGH I SPEAK WITH TONGUES

"That's given us a great start," says Marian. "Now Henrietta, or Clare, have you anything to add? – Henrietta . . ."

"I also have been giving a lot of thought to the great commandment that Marlise has been talking about, but the thing that's been in my mind all the week is this. We think an awful lot about having great gifts such as speaking in tongues like Oral Roberts, or preaching like Billy Graham, or being great Bible scholars like Dr. Paul Rees, or having great faith like George Muller, but all these great things seem so far from ordinary people like us, but then here's this wonderful chapter which shows us how we can serve God in a more excellent way – 1 Corinthians 13 – and God has reminded me that it's not my talents, or my work, but it's my love He wants, and it's these first three verses that have helped me so much.

" 'Though I speak with the tongues of men and of angels, and have not charity, I am become as sounding brass, or a tinkling cymbal. And though I have the gift of prophecy, and understand all mysteries, and all knowledge; and though I have all faith, so that I could remove mountains, and have not charity, I am nothing. And though I bestow all my goods to feed the poor, and though I give my body to be burned, and have not charity, it profiteth me nothing.'

"The only other thought I had was that love is very important because it is the badge, or the sign, of belonging to the Lord, as it says in John 13 verse 35:

" 'By this shall all men know that ye are my disciples, if ye have love one to another.' "

"And have you got anything to add, Clare?" asks Marion.

Clare, a shy woman, says, "No, I think Marlise and Henrietta have really answered the question very well. The more we love anyone, the more we want them to love us, so God must love us a lot to put 'love me' at the top of the commandments."

Marion does not speak, but her eyes say, 'Has anyone anything to say?'

Loeen Sacks speaks up. "I think we all feel that love is very important, but so far we have only been talking about our love for

God, and our love for one another, but surely God's love for us is far more important because without His loving us, we should never really love one another. And also what I would like to know is: just *what* is love?"

"Well, you won't have to wait long for that," says Marion, "because that really is question no. 2. So let's go on to that now. Joanna Stowall, you lead off, and then we'll ask Genevieve Kerr and Anita Randall who also have this question, to follow on."

Joanna; "Question no. 2 is 'How would you define New Testament Christian Love?' And this I have found very difficult to answer. I wish that Marion had given us her introduction last week, because what she said just now has helped me no end, especially that bit about love is an attitude of mind which always tries to say and do the things that will help and bring happiness to those whom we are commanded to love. I must say I've been a bit muddled in my thinking this week. My heart knows what love is, but my brain can't find the right thoughts, nor my tongue the right words to describe it. However, I have found two verses which I hope shed a little light on the question in 1 John 3 verses 16 and 17:

> " 'By this we know love, that he laid down his life for us; and we ought to lay down our lives for the brethren. But if any one has the world's goods, and sees his brother in need, yet closes his heart against him, how does God's love abide in him?'

"From this I would define Christian love as that which shares all its possessions with others, and is prepared to sacrifice itself, even unto death for their good.

"The other verse which has helped me is from the lips of the Lord Jesus Himself in the 14th of John: 'If you love me, you will keep my commandments. . . . He who has my commandments and keeps them, he it is who loves me. . . . If a man loves me, he will keep my word, and my Father will love him. . . . He who does not love me does not keep my words.' It seems from these words that love is not *feeling*, but *doing*, not *emotion*, but *action*. And if I were asked what does it mean to love Christ? I should say it just means obeying Him. And likewise I love my fellow Christians, my neighbours, or my enemies not when I feel sentimental about them, but when I stop saying unkind, untrue and unnecessary things about them, and purpose in my heart and mind to say and do only those positive things which will contribute towards their lasting happiness. But I am afraid I have not been very helpful. I hope Anita and Genevieve will do better."

Marion: "Thank you. Someone once said, 'Love can only be known by the actions which it prompts.' Now Anita, can you help us?"

"Sorry," says Anita, "but I just couldn't get any answer to the question at all. I feel rather like the old lady from Scotland who said, 'It's better felt than telt!' There's a passage here in I Corinthians which I have been thinking about, but it is really more of a *description* of love than a *definition*. I am reading from J. B. Phillips:

" 'This love of which I speak is slow to lose patience – it looks for a way of being constructive. It is not possessive: it is neither anxious to impress nor does it cherish inflated ideas of its own importance. Love has good manners and does not pursue selfish advantage. It is not touchy. It does not compile statistics of evil or gloat over the wickedness of other people. On the contrary, it is glad with all good men when Truth prevails. Love knows no limit to its endurance.' "

Genevieve: "Like Anita I have tried in vain to get a proper definition of love. I asked my husband, Hal, and he said that Dr. R. A. Torrey used to say 'Love is a burning desire for another's good and happiness' and I can't do better than Dr. Torrey!"

THE THIRD QUESTION

"And if no one can do better," says Marion, "let's leave the definition like that and go straight on to the next question no. 3, which I gave to our hostess Martha Amhurst, Maralyn Olsen and Georgina Bushman. Which of you three will lead off? You will Georgina, all right."

"Question no. 3," says Georgina, "asks 'Who ought we to love?' I think Marion gave me this question because it's so much easier than the first two. I suppose this question can be answered in one word 'Everyone', but since this is a Bible Study, I have been looking up various verses for an answer, and first of all this is the answer which the Lord Himself gave in Matthew chapter 22, to which Marlise has already referred under question no. 1. I didn't know till this week that in using these words the Lord was Himself quoting from Deuteronomy chapter 6 verse 5. Above everyone and everything else we are to love God, and our love for

Him is to be all embracing – heart, soul, mind and strength. We are to love Him with *every* motive, emotion, thought and action.

"The second answer I have is also in this same chapter, verse 39 – 'Thou shalt love thy neighbour as thyself.' Whereas God demands 100 per cent of my love, I am to share on a 50/50 basis with my neighbour. It seems that until we really start loving God as we ought, we shall not be able to love others as we ought. The more love I give to God, so the more do I have for others. Perhaps I could draw here on my personal experience.

"As some of you know I have only recently become a Christian. I wasn't against God. I was just completely indifferent to Him, and looking back now, I think I was the most selfish woman in the world. I loved myself most of all, and after that, in a selfish way, I loved my own family and a few carefully selected friends who in various ways ministered to me, but beyond that, the rest of mankind could go hang as far as I was concerned, and then about a year ago through the kindness of Jane Crowther I started coming to these Coffee Mornings, and gradually, in answer to your prayers, and through reading the Bible, I came to see that it was my sin and selfishness which caused Christ to die for me, and this melted my hard and selfish heart, and as I started to love Him, I found myself loving others – selfishness is giving way to consideration, covetousness to generosity, and whereas before I only wanted others to minister to me, now I want to minister to others."

"Thank you, Georgina," says Marion. "A word of practical testimony is always welcome. And now over to Martha or Maralyn, please."

"Well," says Martha, "I have been asking the Lord all the week 'Who ought I to love?' and I have been unable to get away from the Lord's own word which I have found here in Matthew chapter 5, verses 43 and 44:

" 'Ye have heard that it hath been said, Thou shalt love thy neighbour, and hate thine enemy. But I say unto you, Love your enemies, bless them that curse you, do good to them that hate you, and pray for them which despitefully use you, and persecute you.'

I can see something in loving my neighbour, but this idea of loving my enemies has really foxed me, but I must say that I have got a lot of light on it already here this morning.

"Earlier this week I came across two helpful verses in Romans chapter 12, 20 and 21:

66

" Therefore if thine enemy hunger, feed him; if he thirst, give him drink: for in so doing thou shalt heap coals of fire on his head. Be not overcome of evil, but overcome evil with good.'

and I wondered what would happen to an enemy of mine if I cremated him, and suddenly I realised he would be completely destroyed, he would cease to exist and you can't hate someone who doesn't exist. And all this week I have been praying 'O Lord, help me to destroy all my enemies by cremating them with the burning coals of earnest prayers, loving hospitality, kind deeds, and thus help me to remake them as my friends."

And here Maralyn joins in. "I have been able to find several verses telling us whom we should love. Georgina and Martha have already referred to our responsibility to love God, our neighbours and our enemies, but the Bible also teaches us to love our husbands (Ephesians 5: 25), and as Marion has already told us, this is *agapē* not *eros*! We must also love those who are lost:

" 'I say the truth in Christ, I lie not, my conscience also bearing me witness in the Holy Ghost, that I have great heaviness and continual sorrow in my heart. For I could wish that myself were accursed from Christ for my brethren, my kinsmen according to the flesh. . . . Brethren, my heart's desire and prayer to God for Israel is, that they might be saved.' – Romans 9: 1–3; 10: 1.

"Our love for the lost must not stop at heaviness and sorrow of heart, but, like Paul, we must be ready to sacrifice in order to win others by deeds of kindness, earnest prayer, and effective witness."

THE FOURTH QUESTION

"My! how time flies!" exclaims Marion, glancing at her watch. "We must push on with question no. 4. Let's see, this time it's Jane Crowther, Gloria Putnum and Loeen Sacks, and since you are our pastor's wife, Gloria, perhaps you will lead off?"

"O.K," says Gloria, "here's question no. 4. 'What is the source of Christian love, or what is the secret of loving?' This is an important question for us all. Whereas *eros* and affection for our family and friends come fairly naturally to us, we must remember that Christian love – *agapē* – which loves even the unlovely, is completely foreign. Indeed, Paul tells us that by nature we were hateful, and hating one another:

67

" 'For we ourselves also were sometimes foolish, disobedient, deceived, serving divers lusts and pleasures, living
in malice and envy, hateful, and hating one another' –
Titus 3: 3.

The secret spring of this divine love is not in us, but in God Himself. As John says 'Love is of God' and 'God is love', but let me
read the passage from 1 John 4, verses 7, 8, 10, 11:

" 'Beloved, let us love one another: for love is of God;
and every one that loveth is born of God, and knoweth God.
He that loveth not knoweth not God: for God is love. . . .
Herein is love, not that we loved God, but that he loved
us, and sent his Son to be the propitiation for our sins.
Beloved, if God so loved us, we ought also to love one
another.'

"Here John answers question no. 4 for us – God Himself is
the source of Christian love, and the secret of our loving is to be
found in being born again by God, so that as His children, we
know Him, and are partakers of His divine nature. Moreover His
love towards us, manifested in the death of His Son, begets love
in us for Him – 'we love Him, because He first loved us' verse 19
– and for one another, St. Paul says the same thing in different
words in Romans chapter 5 verses 5–8:

" 'the love of God is shed abroad in our hearts by the
Holy Ghost which is given unto us. For when we were
yet without strength, in due time Christ died for the
ungodly. For scarcely for a righteous man will one die: yet
peradventure for a good man some would even dare to die.
But God commendeth His love toward us, in that, while we
were yet sinners, Christ died for us.' "

THE FRUIT OF THE SPIRIT

And here Loeen takes up the question. "Yes, for my answer I
went to Galatians chapter 5 verse 22 – 'But the fruit of the Spirit
is love' – the Holy Spirit Himself is the root and source of Christian love. Then I thought of the Master's own words in Matthew
chapter 7 verses 16b–18:

" 'Do men gather grapes of thorns, or figs of thistles?
Even so every good tree bringeth forth good fruit; but a
corrupt tree bringeth forth evil fruit. A good tree cannot
bring forth evil fruit, neither can a corrupt tree bring
forth good fruit.'

Grapes of thorns, or figs of thistles

"Our hearts are naturally corrupt and poisonous like thorns and thistles, but when God by His Spirit makes the tree good, then we bring forth the good fruit of Christian love."

And Jane follows on: "My answer is similar to your's, Loeen, but I have been thinking about the Parable of the Vine in John 15. There's not time to read it all, but here are some of the verses which help to answer the question:

> " 'I am the true vine, and my Father is the husbandman. . . . Abide in me, and I in you. As the branch cannot bear fruit of itself, except it abide in the vine; no more can ye, except ye abide in me. I am the vine, ye are the branches: He that abideth in me, and I in him, the same bringeth forth much fruit: for without me ye can do nothing. . . . Herein is my Father glorified, that ye bear much fruit; so shall ye be my disciples. As the Father hath loved me, so have I loved you: continue ye in my love. . . . This is my commandment, That ye love one another, as I have loved you.' "

"I have a question I'd like to put to the group," says Lois Schneider. "I am sure that I am a child of God, but I find it very difficult to maintain this Christian love that we have been talking about. Can anyone help?"

A moment's silence, then Clare Aitkinson says:

"I find that my love for God and others is only maintained and increased through my private prayers every day. I have to pray the prayer Paul offered on behalf of the Christians in Philippi:

> " 'And this I pray, that your love may abound yet more and more in knowledge and in all judgment.' "

"And not only prayer," says Marlise Hoffman, "but also the Word of God. Here are three scriptures which I always link up:

" 'Whereby are given unto us exceeding great and precious promises: that by these ye might be partakers of the divine nature.' – 2 Peter 1: 4a.

'This book of the law shall not depart out of thy mouth; but thou shalt meditate therein day and night, that thou mayest observe to do according to all that is written therein: for then thou shalt make thy way prosperous, and then thou shalt have good success.' – Joshua 1: 8.

'But his delight is in the law of the Lord; and in his law doth he meditate day and night. And he shall be like a tree planted by the rivers of water, that bringeth forth his fruit in his season; his leaf also shall not wither; and whatsoever he doeth shall prosper.' " – Ps. 1: 2, 3.

"Sorry!" says Marion, "Time's up! We must save the last few minutes for prayer on this important topic. I am sure you all realise that we have only just started on this great theme of the love of God, but we have at any rate covered the four questions I set out last week. Now those who want to continue the study privately at home, you might like to jot down some of the other questions I have here on the same subject. 'What does the Bible teach about the Father's love for His Son?' 'In what practical ways should our love for Christ be seen?' 'Is the love of God for the sinner the same as His love for His children?' 'In what ways does God manifest His love toward us?' 'Several scriptures exhort us to imitate God's love, can you find the references?' 'The Gospels name several persons whom Jesus loved. Who were they?' 'In what specific ways should our love for others manifest itself?' "

And here, Mr. Reader, we must say 'farewell' to Marion and her Bible Cell.

What other themes can I recommend for this type of subject study? Yes, I'll gladly make some suggestions; but first, please let me urge you to select themes that your Cell will be able to understand and enjoy, and take them in by the shallow end. Here then are some suggested subjects which I am setting out in alphabetical order:

Angels	Eternal Life	Grace
Atonement	Faith	Growth
The Bible	Forgiveness	Heaven
The Church	Giving	Hell
Conscience	The Gospel	The Holy Spirit

Inspiration	Regeneration	Service
John the Baptist	Repentance	Sin
Judgment	Restitution	Substitution
Justification	Salvation	The Trinity
Peace	Sanctification	Walking
Reconciliation	Satan	The World
Redemption	The Scriptures	Worship

Many other subjects will be found listed in any good reference Bible. Here may I recommend a good Bible Subject Study Book, useful for new disciples, produced many years ago by a good friend of mine, the late R. T. Archibald, entitled *The Spirit's Sword*.*

Bible Cells are not in any sense a substitute for either the public proclamation of the Gospel or the authoritative exposition of the Word of God. There are many Bible passages – indeed whole books – which do not lend themselves to any method of group study. They call for special handling by a spiritually minded well-taught, gifted expositor, and although these men are few and far between in these days of apostasy, thank God they are still to be found.

Bible Cell members should never look upon their group studies as a substitute for the private, personal study of Scripture.

Since I have been leading verse-by-verse Bible Studies at Hildenborough conferences since 1945, literally thousands of individual people have come to me expressing their amazement: "I had no idea there was so much in the Bible." "I have learnt exactly how it is that God speaks to people through the Bible." "My Bible will become a new book to me as a result of this session." "I have read that passage many times before, and had no idea there was so much in it." "This has been one of my most exciting spiritual experiences." "I am going away to study my Bible with a new enthusiasm."

This verse-by-verse method of Bible Study has been adopted by Christian leaders throughout the world, and is used today by countless Christian people in their own devotional studies.

* *The Spirit's Sword* by R. T. Archibald. 44 pages, price 3s. 6d. (50c (postage and packing extra), The Bookroom, Hildenborough Hall, Otford Hills Sevenoaks, Kent, England.

Understanding the Bible

TO SOME people the Bible is dead, irrelevant, and little short of boring, whilst to others it is living, practical, and fascinating. How then is the Bible to become interesting, relevant, and challenging to a Bible Cell? The important part of the answer to this question can be given in one stark word – OBEDIENCE.

Amongst the important lesser-known sayings of our Lord is one hidden away in the 7th chapter of John which every Bible Cell would do well to consider carefully:

> If any man will do His (God's) Will, he shall know of the doctrine. – John 7: 17.

In these words our Lord lays down a vital principle of spiritual perception and understanding. We often argue: "If only I knew and understood Bible doctrine fully, I would then make a complete dedication of my life to God" – but our Lord reverses this order. He says that if we are willing to do what God says, then our willing obedience will result in spiritual understanding and perception. In other words, the secret of understanding the Word of God is to be found in obeying it honestly and instantly as it is revealed to us. When God speaks to us, we must believe and obey Him without question, and if we do this we shall find that the next time He speaks we shall understand His Word more readily. If, on the other hand, when God speaks, we disobey Him, or ignore His Word, then immediately we will start to lose our spiritual perception and understanding:

> Who hath ears to hear, let him hear. . . . For whosoever hath, to him shall be given, and he shall have more abundance: but whosoever hath not, from him shall be taken away even that he hath. – Matthew 13: 9, 12.

Yes, obedience to the Word is the secret of enjoying it and understanding it. This principle is true, not only for the individual Christian, but for every Bible Cell.

Sam is a radiant Christian man, a member of a coloured Church in the Deep South. He has a great reverence for the Word of God. He reads his Bible daily on his knees. No, I am sure he doesn't worship the Bible, but he does worship the God Who speaks to him through the Bible. Some might say that his approach to the Scriptures is a little naïve, but knowing him as I do, I would say that it is childlike. The Bible seems to present no problems to Sam whatever. "The parts of the Bible that I find difficult, Dr. Rees, are not the parts that I do *not* understand, but the parts that I *do* understand," he told me recently. A while ago a scholarly theologian of the Reformed Tradition was talking to Sam.

"Tell me," he said, "what do you make of this passage in Romans 8 – 'Whom he did foreknow, he also did predestinate?' "

"There's no problem there at all," said Sam with a smile. "This is how you understand that passage. You start at Matthew chapter 1, and do all the dear Lord tells you to do there, then you comes to the Sermon on the Mount, and you do all the dear Lord tells you to do there, and you go right through the four Gospels, then the Acts, doing whatever the Lord tells you to do without arguing, and by the time you comes to Romans chapter 8, that passage is quite simple!"

The same sun that hardens the clay, melts the wax; the same Bible which is lifeless and dead to one Bible Cell, is living and active to another. The former group come to the Bible to criticise the Bible; the latter come to the Bible to be criticised by the Bible. The former Group merely discuss the Bible; the latter translate it into action and character.

MOTIVE FOR BIBLE STUDY

Every individual Christian, and certainly every Bible Cell, before reading or studying God's Word, should ask themselves these questions: "What is my motive? Am I studying God's Word just because it interests me? Because I want to become a better teacher or preacher? Because I want to impress others with my knowledge of the Word? Because I want to become a more effective Christian worker?" These motives are utterly unworthy. Our main objects in studying the Scriptures should be that we may come to know and love the Lord Jesus better; that our faith and confidence in Him may grow; that we may know His Will in order that we might do it.

> This book of the law shall not depart out of thy mouth; but thou shalt meditate therein day and night, *that thou mayest observe to do according to all that is written therein:* for then thou shalt make thy way prosperous, and then thou shalt have good success. – Joshua 1: 8.

My wife, Jean, was present at a verse-by-verse Bible Study

where the group were going through the first Epistle of John. They came to the verse:

My little children, let us not love in word, neither in tongue; but in deed and in truth. – 1 John 3: 18.

After discussing it for a while, a rather shy person turned to the leader and said:

"Do you not think that as fellow Christians we should take these words to heart, and see that from henceforth we love one another in a more practical way?"

The leader looked up at him with a frown on his face, and replied:

"That remark is completely out of place. We are here for the study of Scripture, not for exhortation."

Impression without expression leads to depression. When God speaks to an individual, or a group, and His Word is obeyed, the Bible springs to life, and the heart is filled with joy, but when God speaks and His command goes unheeded, the Bible ceases to live, and the heart loses its song.

I remember that radiant Christian, Miss Ruth Paxson, telling us how she was seeking to help a Christian girl who, like Peter, was following the Lord afar off. They were reading Matthew's Gospel and praying together. They came to chapter 28, verse 17:

And when they saw Him, they worshipped Him: but some doubted.

Miss Paxson read the Word, and then both she and the girl, the obedient and the disobedient Christian, spoke at once. "No wonder they worshipped," exclaimed Miss Paxson. "No wonder they doubted," said the girl.

Now I am sorry to labour this point, but the importance of this truth cannot be over-emphasised. The spiritual life of every Bible Cell is utterly dependent upon the practical obedience that the members individually, and the Cell collectively, give to the Word of God. Believe and obey what God reveals to you, and your fellowship will be warm, your Bibles will sparkle, and your witness will be effective. Overlook the practical application of the Word of God in your daily lives, and your fellowship will become formal, your Bibles dead, and your witness utterly barren. No matter what chapter, what subject, or verse you are studying, let all members of the Cell ask themselves these vital questions – "What command is there here that I can obey?" "How can I translate this Scripture into practical action, godly conversation, and Christlike character?"

Supposing your group is making a verse-by-verse study of the Sermon on the Mount, and you come across this paragraph:

> If thou bring thy gift to the altar, and there rememberest that thy brother hath ought against thee; leave there thy gift before the altar, and go thy way; first be reconciled to thy brother, and then come and offer thy gift. – Matthew 5: 23, 24.

These verses present you with a unique opportunity of displaying your profound knowledge of the book of Leviticus, and showing your fellow members how well taught you are in the types, but may be the Holy Spirit reminds you as you meditate that, mainly due to your own fault, you are at variance with a fellow Christian. What are you going to do? Impress the other members of your Cell with your knowledge of the Word, or bow your head in silent prayer, and say: "Lord, I'll call in on my friend on the way home tonight and apologise for my rudeness." This is the Bible in action; this is the way of faith, perception, and spiritual development. This is the way of Life.

Or supposing your group is considering Romans 13, and you come to the paragraph:

> For for this cause pay ye tribute also: for they are God's ministers, attending continually upon this very thing. Render therefore to all their dues: tribute to whom tribute is due; custom to whom custom; fear to whom fear; honour to whom honour. Owe no man any thing, but to love one another: for he that loveth another hath fulfilled the law. – Romans 13: 6–8.

and as you look at these practical exhortations, you remember that last year you did not make a full and honest declaration of your income to the Tax Authorities or you recall that when you came home from abroad last summer, you deliberately brought in some taxable goods without declaring them to the Customs Officer; or you remember that bill which is still outstanding to one of the local tradespeople which through slackness you have not paid. Now, what are you going to do? Ignore God's Word? If so, this will spell death to your own spiritual life, and to that of your Cell, but pay those taxes, that duty, or the bill, and God will bless you and the group, and next week the Bible will become a new Book.

To study the Bible just for the sake of studying the Bible is not only a waste of time, but highly dangerous.

But be ye doers of the Word, and not hearers only, deceiving your own selves. For if any be a hearer of the Word, and not a doer, he is like unto a man beholding his natural face in a glass: for he beholdeth himself, and goeth his way, and straightway forgetteth what manner of man he was. But whoso looketh into the perfect law of liberty, and continueth therein, he being not a forgetful hearer, but a doer of the work, this man shall be blessed in his deed. – James 1 : 22–25.

Some Cells make it a rule that at the end of each Bible Study they will not leave the passage until they have come up with a 'project' – that is, they agree as to what practical action they will take as a result of their study. Sometimes this 'project' is decided on by the group, and sometimes each member names his own 'project'.

PARALLEL SCRIPTURES

Beyond doubt the best commentary on the Bible is the Bible itself. In seeking to understand God's Word we should read it reverently on our knees, at the same time praying earnestly that just as God sent Philip, the Evangelist, to help the man of Ethiopia understand the Scripture, so should He send the Holy Spirit to be our Teacher and Guide. (See Acts 8: 26–40 and John 14: 26.)

Then having prayed and meditated carefully upon the passage, we should search diligently for other verses or paragraphs in the Bible which might shed further light on the passage under consideration. These verses are known as cross references, or parallel passages. We should then read the passage in some other version, or versions, than the one to which we are accustomed to using, and then – only then – having prayed and compared Scripture with Scripture, should we turn to the Commentaries. Alas, there are many ministers, evangelists, and teachers who, whenever they are faced with a verse or passage of Scripture reach immediately for their favourite Commentary, and thus they give the Holy Spirit very little, if any, opportunity of teaching them directly from the Word of truth. These people are rather like the housewife who always reaches for the can opener because she is too lazy to buy and prepare fresh food for the family. Don't misunderstand me, I believe in good Bible Commentaries as much as anyone; indeed, my library shelves are full of them, but for many years I have disciplined myself first to pray, then to read, then compare Scripture with Scripture, then meditate, and finally read what God has previously taught His other servants.

Martin Luther said: "That is the true method of interpretation, which puts Scripture alongside of Scripture in a right and proper way."

John Wesley, who was himself converted through the writings of Luther, wrote: "Here then I am, far from the busy ways of men. I sit down alone: only God is here. In His presence I open, I read His book; for this end, to find the way to heaven. Is there a doubt concerning the meaning of what I read? Does anything appear dark and intricate? I lift up my heart to the Father of Lights: Lord, is it not Thy word, 'If any man lack wisdom, let him ask of God'? Thou 'givest liberally and upbraidest not'. Thou hast said, 'If any be willing to do Thy will, he shall know'. I am willing to do, let me know Thy will. I then search after and consider parallel passages of Scripture, comparing spiritual things with spiritual. I meditate thereon with all the attention and earnestness of which my mind is capable. If any doubt still remains, I consult those who are experienced in the things of God; and then the writings whereby, being dead, they yet speak. And what I thus learn, that I teach."

A CHAIN OF VERSES

I am deeply indebted to my brother, Dick, who, when I first became a Christian, taught me how to use my Bible, comparing one passage with another. In those days when we were walking to a meeting (only the rich owned cars in the 1920s!) one of us would say, "Let's forge a chain of Bible verses. You start tonight, Jim." And Jim would forge the first link. "All we like sheep have gone astray; we have turned every one to his own way; and the Lord hath laid on him the iniquity of us all – Isa. 53:6." Without hesitation the next man was ready with the second link: "For ye were as sheep going astray; but are now returned unto the Shepherd and Bishop of your souls – 1 Peter 2:25;" and then the third: "I am the good shepherd: the good shepherd giveth his life for the sheep – John 10:11." The next man followed on with what we called a weak link, because he did not know the reference. "The Son of man came not to be ministered unto, but to minister, and to give his life a ransom for many – sorry I don't know the reference, but think it's somewhere in Matthew." Dick strengthened the link. "Yes, it's in chapter 20, I think it's verse 28," then the next link was forged – "For the Son of man is come to seek and to save that which was lost" – Luke 19:10. And so on.

We had rules for these chains which included the following:

1. No verse must be repeated in a chain.

2. Not more than two consecutive links were to be on the same subject. For instance, having started with Isaiah 53: 6, the second link 1 Peter 2: 25 was forged out of the phrase, "All we like sheep have gone astray". If, therefore, the third link had been suggested as "All have sinned and come short of the glory of God", that link would have been rejected.

3. Contrast verses were also permissible. For instance, if one quoted: "He that is not with me is against me" – Matt. 12: 30, another could follow on with – "He that is not against us is for us" – Luke 9: 50.

Sometimes by way of variety one of us would name a text which we would call the basic text, and then we would see how many relevant Scriptures we could quote arising from that one verse. For instance, if someone suggested as the basic text Isaiah 43: 1: "But now thus saith the Lord that created thee, O Jacob, and he that formed thee, O Israel, Fear not: for I have redeemed thee, I have called thee by thy name; thou art Mine," we would then go to work and rack our brains for every Scripture where God is referred to as our Creator, and then we would move on to every verse we could think of where we are exhorted to fear not, and then on to the subject of redemption, then to the many verses where God called people by name, and finally to the parallel verses on the phrase: "Thou art Mine." Very often we would engage in this spiritual, intellectual exercise for more than an hour at a stretch. It not only encouraged us to memorise Scripture, but gave us an idea how to compare spiritual things with spiritual.

SPIRITUAL EXERCISE

It would be a good thing if, in your Cell, from time to time, you devoted ten or fifteen minutes to these spiritual exercises. You will find these verse chains not only entertaining, but also a good investment of time, for there are many parts of the Bible which can only be understood in the light of other passages. Let me give you three examples: Exodus 12 and 1 Peter 1; Exodus 16 and John 6; Isaiah 53 and 1 Peter 2: 21 ff. Our Lord Himself, when preaching and teaching, constantly quoted relevant passages from Moses, the Psalms and the Prophets. His students, the Apostles, followed His wise example. For instance, Matthew in his Gospel quotes no less than fifty-three passages of Old Testament Scripture.

The most virile Cells are those who use the Bible constantly as their authoritative commentary. Many Bibles give marginal references of useful parallel verses and passages. Alas, some people are just too lazy to turn the pages!

Whilst using parallel Scriptures in Group Studies, care should be taken to see that the study does not deteriorate into a competition as to who knows his Bible best. Only parallel passages which shed clear light on the passage or subject under consideration should be quoted.

Apart from the Bible itself, I think the most valuable book I have in my library is one which I bought soon after my conversion, entitled *The Treasury of Scripture Knowledge* which gives 500,000 Scripture references and parallel passages, arranged under chapter and verse to suit any version of the Bible.*

Bible Commentaries are, of course, exceedingly helpful, particularly in giving local background and the derivation and meaning of words.

In his preparation the appointed leader, having prayed, compared Scripture with Scripture, and meditated upon the passage, should most certainly read every good Commentary available to him, but neither he nor members of the Cell should bring Commentaries to the Group Bible Studies.

PASSAGES FOR STUDY

Both the passages of Scripture which were used at Warren Farm and the Teenagers' Cell were those which readily lent themselves to the verse-by-verse method of study. If your Cell consists only of mature Christians and experienced Bible Students, then by all means study the meatier Scriptures, but it is of the utmost importance that every newly formed Bible Cell, and those consisting mainly of new disciples, or young people, should concentrate on elementary Bible passages which are more easily understood.

At their first meeting, one Cell of beginners discussed which book they should first study together, and finally agreed upon the book of Revelation, taking it verse by verse through the twenty-two chapters; moreover, they decided that every meeting would be a Bible Study. Needless to say the numbers dwindled, and the Cell died a natural death. A kindergarten teacher does not start with long division when teaching arithmetic! A mother does not feed her newborn baby on a diet of steak and oysters! There are

* *The Treasury of Scripture Knowledge*, 500,000 Scripture references and parallel passages. Fleming H. Revell Company, Westwood, N.J., U.S.A. Samuel Bagster & Sons Limited, London; 30s. (postage and packing extra). The Bookroom, Hildenborough Hall, Otford Hills, Sevenoaks, Kent, England.

many passages (as I have already pointed out) which do not lend themselves to the verse-by-verse method, or any other form of group study. These Scriptures can only be handled adequately by a spiritually minded, well taught, gifted expositor. Group Bible Study is not a substitute, but a stimulant to the public exposition of the Word.

If you are forming a new Bible Cell, call your key people together, and pray for the guidance of the Spirit, then decide together how many meetings you are going to have in your first series of studies, then the passages of Scripture you plan to study. Rather than starting off with a series from a particular book of the Bible, you should, during your first term, select a series of eight or twelve elementary passages which readily lend themselves to group study. Here is a list of such Scriptures which might prove helpful.

Milk of the Word

ELEMENTARY PASSAGES

Abraham offering Isaac	Genesis 22: 1–14
Isaac and Rebekah	Genesis 24: 1–67
The Passover	Exodus 12: 1–14
The Manna	Exodus 16: 1–36
The Brazen Serpent	Numbers 21: 4–10
Rahab of Jericho	Joshua 2: 1–24
Caleb	Joshua 14: 1–15
Jephthah	Judges 11: 1–33
David and Mephibosheth	2 Samuel 9: 1–13

The Barrel of Meal	1 Kings 17: 8–16
*Naaman the Leper	2 Kings 5: 1–14
Four Starving Lepers	2 Kings 7: 1–20
Valley of Dry Bones	Ezekiel 37: 1–10
A Roman Officer's Faith	Matthew 8: 5–13
Death of John Baptist	Matthew 14: 1–14
*Peter Walks on the Water	Matthew 14: 22–33
Marriage of the King's Son	Matthew 22: 1–14
*Man Sick of the Palsy	Mark 2: 3–12
The Legion of Demons	Mark 5: 1–20
*Blind Bartimaeus	Mark 10: 46–52
The Colt Tied	Mark 11: 1–11
*Fishers of Men	Luke 5: 1–11
The Good Samaritan	Luke 10: 25–37
Martha and Mary	Luke 10: 38–42
Ten Lepers Cleansed	Luke 17: 11–19
*Zacchaeus	Luke 19: 1–10
The Walk to Emmaus	Luke 24: 13–35
Personal Evangelism	John 1: 29–51
Water Turned to Wine	John 2: 1–12
The Woman of Samaria	John 4: 5–26
The Nobleman's Son	John 4: 46–54
The Pool of Bethesda	John 5: 1–18
*The Feeding of the Five Thousand	John 6: 1–14
The Man Born Blind	John 9: 1–41
The Good Shepherd	John 10: 1–18
The Raising of Lazarus	John 11: 1–46
The Feast at Bethany	John 12: 1–11
The True Vine	John 15: 1–17
Thomas the Doubter	John 20: 19–31
The Multitude of Fishes	John 21: 1–14
*The Lame Man	Acts 3: 1–11
The Ethiopian Eunuch	Acts 8: 26–40
The Conversion of Saul	Acts 9: 1–19
Peter brought out of Prison	Acts 12: 1–19
The Jailer at Philippi	Acts 16: 25–34

ELEMENT OF SURPRISE

Opinions differ as to whether or not it is advisable to announce in advance the passage which is to be studied in the group. Some Cells with whom I have discussed the matter feel very strongly that the passage should be announced in advance, giving the

* These passages are particularly suitable for beginners.

members time to read, meditate, pray, and study the passage, but the majority of groups who use the verse-by-verse method have discovered that it is better for the passage to be announced only when the group comes together for study. This gives an element of surprise, and prevents some of the more talkative members from preparing sermonettes on the passage, or merely repeating what they have read in their commentaries during the past week.

If the Cell is doing a course of studies, it is perhaps better that passages be announced in advance, but there is no set rule about this matter.

New Cells would be well advised to do a little experimenting along this line. The fresher we are when we approach the passage, the better. Leading verse-by-verse Bible Studies for ministers and evangelists is never easy. Each man produces his own sermon and the study is stillborn! The most original thoughts and refreshing studies often come from teenage groups.

BOOK BY BOOK

When the 'basic' passages have been studied, provided the members of the Cell are showing signs of spiritual growth and development, the Scriptures selected for study should be based upon a single book of the Bible. This will make for spiritual maturity by providing a balanced diet of doctrine.

Only in exceptional circumstances should a Cell attempt to go through an entire book verse by verse and chapter by chapter. The majority of people do not have the spiritual or intellectual capacity for an exhaustive study of a complete book. Remember that the speed of a convoy is always determined by the slowest moving vessel.

But having said this, I want to make it clear that no one believes more in the study of complete books of the Bible than I; indeed, to my mind this is the only really satisfactory method of studying the Bible, but it should be undertaken by an individual, not by a group.

One Cell that had been formed a considerable time decided to go through the Psalter, Psalm by Psalm. After eight months of hard labour, during which time several promising young disciples gave up the ghost, they realised their error and switched to another book, only just in time to save the life of the Cell. They should have selected certain more suitable Psalms for their studies rather than attempt the complete book. After all the main purpose of group Bible Study is not to make an exhaustive study of Scripture, but rather to give Christian people the desire and the know-how to search the Scriptures privately for themselves. If I were asked to plan a series of studies in the Book of Psalms, I think I would make my selection from the following:

Psalm 1, 2, 3, 8, 14, 16, 19, 22, 23, 24, 27, 32, 34, 37, 40, 46, 51, 63, 84, 90, 91, 95, 103, 121, 139, 146.

Now suppose a Cell of more experienced Christians decide to study various books of the Bible, in which order should they proceed? I put this question recently to two friends of mine, both of whom are first-class scholars and eminent Bible students – John Taylor, Vice-Principal of Oakhill Theological College, London, and Donald Guthrie of The London Bible College.

John Taylor suggests that if there are people in a Cell who are not thoroughly well acquainted with the main events in the life of our Lord, they would be well advised to start with Mark's Gospel, for it is short, and full of life and movement. Next they should turn to John's Gospel, for this is the seeker's book, and highlights the great themes about the Person of our Lord. After studying these two Gospels, John Taylor suggests that the Cell should stay in the New Testament, moving on to Philippians, 1 Timothy, 1 Peter, and 1 John, then back to the Old Testament.

Donald Guthrie also suggests that a Cell should start their book studies with Mark's Gospel, as he thinks it serves as an excellent introduction to the other three Gospels, and lays great stress on the activities of our Lord. This should be followed by John's Gospel, which introduces more of the teachings of Christ. Before proceeding to the Epistles, he thinks it would be valuable to make a study of the book of the Acts since this book is a natural bridge between the Gospels and the Epistles. After the Acts, he recommends Philippians, Colossians, and 1 Corinthians, then 1 Peter, 1 John, and James.

For studies in Old Testament books, Donald Guthrie recommends starting with key chapters in Genesis and Exodus as they are obviously foundation books. These should be followed, he thinks, by the Psalms, then the historical books Samuel, Kings, Joshua, and Judges, followed by Ezra and Nehemiah.

STUDIES IN JOHN

Suppose, when you have been going a while, your Bible Cell decides to base its studies on John's Gospel. Let the leaders, or one or two more experienced students, meet together and plan prayerfully a syllabus, selecting certain passages for verse-by-verse study, leaving individuals free to complete in their own homes the study of the chapters or paragraphs that are omitted. They might arrange a series on some of the miracles recorded by John.

Water that was made Wine	2: 1–12
The Nobleman's Son	4: 46–54
The Impotent Man	5: 1–18
Loaves and Fishes	6: 1–14
Jesus Walking on the Sea	6: 15–21
One that was Born Blind	9: 1–41
Lazarus of Bethany	11: 1–46
He is Risen!	20: 1–18
The Net Full	21: 1–14

or, if the Cell is particularly interested in personal evangelism, a series on 'Christ counselling the individual'.

The Apostles	1: 35–51
Nicodemus	3: 1–21
The Women of Sychar	4: 1–45
The Woman taken in Adultery	8: 1–11
Mary Magdalene	20: 1–18
Thomas	20: 19–31

Or, a more advanced group could examine the sermons of Jesus.

All should Honour the Son	5: 19–46
The Bread of Life	6: 25–71
At the Feast of Tabernacles	7: 14–53
The Light of the World	8: 12–59
The Good Shepherd	10: 1–39
To the Greeks	12: 20–50
The True Vine	15: 1–17

A series of eight consecutive studies is ideal. Twelve should be the maximum number. Variety is the spice of life – and it is certainly the spice of group Bible Study. Indeed, the Bible itself is teaming with variety: history, parable, law, poetry, sermons, letters, prophecies, and more beside.

Now, having written extensively on Bible Study, which is the first of the five common characteristics of Bible Cells, we will now consider the second which is:

II. PRAYER

The majority of Bible Cells are formed in the first place for *one* express purpose, either for Bible Study, prayer, fellowship, or evangelism, but whatever the original purpose, if the Cell is really healthy, it is never long before individual members, and sometimes the entire Cell, become deeply concerned about their relations and neighbours who do not know the Saviour. The more we love God, the more we want others to know Him! This is a healthy sign, for salvation is not given to us as a privilege, but is entrusted to us as a solemn responsibility.

> I have chosen you, and ordained you, that ye should go and bring forth fruit, and that your fruit should remain. – John 15: 16.

A most critical phase is reached in the life of a Cell when its members develop this love for souls – this God-given urge to 'reproduce'. One might almost say that the Cell has now entered spiritual adolescence! This stage in development is critical because if this urge is not expressed both in prayer and practical outreach, the life of the Cell will turn in upon itself and stagnate into a 'holy huddle'! One of the Divine principles of spiritual life is that in order to *get*, we must *give*.

> There is that scattereth, and yet increaseth; and there is that withholdeth more than is meet, but it tendeth to poverty. – Proverbs 11: 24.

> For whosoever will save his life shall lose it; and whosoever will lose his life for my sake shall find it. – Matthew 16: 25.

Many a Bible Cell has expired completely, or worse still, become a mere end in itself when, instead of seeking to make Christ known to outsiders, its members have only met to receive help one from another. It is imperative that every individual Christian, every church and Bible Cell should realise that they are here in this world for one express purpose: to glorify God in making Him known to others. The Christian Church is the only institution on earth that exists exclusively for the benefit of non-members! To lose this vision is to perish!

> Ye are my witnesses, saith the Lord, and my servant whom I have chosen. . . . This people have I formed for myself; they shall shew forth my praise.– Isaiah 43: 10a, 21.

> But you are a chosen race. . . . God's own people, that

you may declare the wonderful deeds of him who called
you out of darkness into his marvellous light. – 1 Peter 2: 9.

PAUL'S DESIRE AND PRAYER

When the hearts and minds of Christian people become
possessed by a deep love for souls, the first thing they do is to
pray, both privately, and with their fellow Christians. They
commence to intercede, to pray on behalf of the lost! Few people
have felt this burden, or prayed more earnestly than the Apostle
Paul, and it is significant that he refers to this 'unceasing anguish
and incessant travail' in the same chapter in which he writes of
the Sovereignty of God. Every Christian should ponder his words
carefully:

> For I could wish that myself were accursed from Christ for
> my brethren, my kinsmen according to the flesh. –
> Romans 9: 3.

> Brethren, my heart's desire and prayer to God for Israel
> is, that they might be saved. – Romans 10: 1.

There is nothing which makes us realise our utter impotence
and God's mighty power like a love for souls – and it is this
realisation that drives us to our knees and makes us pray like true
Calvinists. After all, what can *we* do to make a sinner conscious of
his sin, his need of Christ and repentance? And thus in our weakness we cast ourselves upon the grace and generosity of Him
Who alone has power to raise the dead. And it is through this
quality of intercession that souls are conceived and quickened –
and without it, all our preaching, witnessing, organisation, talent,
and evangelistic technique is futile.

I believe that no one is born of God's Spirit unless somebody
somewhere prays for him, not vaguely or generally, but personally
and specifically. Whenever I lead someone to Christ, I always ask
this question.

"Now, tell me, who has been praying for you?"

Back comes the answer at once.

"My mother," "My Minister," "My brother," or "A Christian
in our office."

Joan Windmill, the actress who played in Billy Graham's film
"Souls in Conflict" thought she was the exception to this rule.
She knew no one who could have prayed for her, but she was
wrong! Joan's husband, Bill Brown, met a man in Australia who
told him:

"Some while ago I saw a photo of an actress, Joan Windmill, and felt constrained to pray for her conversion, and this I continued to do for many months, and of course, Joan eventually went to hear Billy Graham preach at Harringay, where she became a Christian."

I feel strongly about this because I owe everything in the spiritual realm to the prayers of others. There was a time in my life, a time of which I am not proud, when I boasted that I was an agnostic. I scoffed at the thought of God, laughed at those who went to church, and poured contempt on people who read the Bible and prayed. My brother Dick, who is a little older than I, and far wiser, turned to Christ when he was a young man, and he became deeply concerned that I too should become a Christian. He tried reasoning and pleading with me, but my response was always the same, laughter and mockery. Then one day he called together a small group of his Christian friends, and told them of his problem. That night before they parted, each one had covenanted to pray for me every day until I committed my life to Jesus Christ. I knew nothing about this conspiracy of prayer, but from that day God started working in my soul, creating a sense of inadequacy and a need of Christ which by and by led to repentance, faith, and new life.

Now, if a Bible Cell is to be virile and effective, its members must learn to intercede on behalf of individual unbelievers among their own relations, neighbours, and workmates. This praying must be with faith and perseverance, in fellowship with other Christians. Moreover, it must not be vague 'for all sorts and conditions of men', but specific – praying for specific men and women *by name* – that in God's own way and time they may be truly converted to Christ. This is how the early Christians prayed, and we must follow the New Testament pattern.

MARY'S BIBLE CELL

One of the many Bible Cells referred to in the New Testament was that held in the home of Mary, the sister of Barnabas and mother of John Mark; and in the twelfth chapter of Acts, Luke gives us a vivid word picture of what this Cell was like, and what Mary and her fellow Christians accomplished through prayer. (This chapter makes an excellent verse-by-verse study under the title 'How to pray effectively for non-Christian friends' – try it in your Cell!)

Peter, a man known personally and loved deeply by members of Mary's Cell, had been taken captive by a cruel foe (Acts 12: 1–4),

A light shined in the prison

put in chains (Acts 12: 6), and was condemned already (Acts 12: 4b).

BUT

But PRAYER

But Prayer WAS MADE

But Prayer was made WITHOUT CEASING

But Prayer was made without ceasing OF THE CHURCH

But Prayer was made without ceasing of the Church UNTO GOD

But Prayer was made without ceasing of the Church unto God FOR HIM

Acts 12: 5.

We too have friends who are taken captive by Satan (2 Timothy 2: 26), enslaved by sin (John 8: 31–34), and are condemned already (John 3: 18, 19).

Humanly speaking Peter was lost and beyond hope, and could do nothing to save himself.

Yes, this New Testament Bible Cell believed in prayer – "But *prayer*." What is more they prayed – "But Prayer *was made*." What is more they prayed with perseverance – "But prayer was made *without ceasing*." What is more they prayed unitedly – "But prayer was made without ceasing *of the church*." What is more they prayed sincerely – "But prayer was made without ceasing of the church *unto God*." What is more they prayed specifically for Peter – "But prayer was made without ceasing of the church unto God *for him.*"

Every Christian believes in prayer, but how few actually pray! Most of us start to pray, but how few pray with perseverance! Undoubtedly, some pray privately for the salvation of their friends, but how rarely do they learn the secret of covenanting with other Christians in prayer! Most praying people pray in a vague way for those who are lost, but few, very few ever learn to pray specifically for people by name! Yes, this is the Biblical method of prayer, the sort of prayer which brings deliverance to the captive.

CONCENTRATED PRAYER

The power of concentrated prayer is immeasurable. Mary and her friends in Jerusalem prayed, not for 'all those in captivity', but specifically for Peter. Have you noticed how Bible prayers are all pointed, personal, and crisp? The bare heat of the sun rarely starts a fire, but take a magnifying glass and concentrate its rays, and in seconds you can start a major conflagration! The vague, general prayers of the average Christian are certainly better than nothing, but the man who concentrates his prayers, faith, and love on an individual kindles a flame of sacred fire, an inextinguishable blaze!

Let each enlightened Christian in every Cell select not less than six, and not more than twenty, people (or families), and major on them in persistent prayer until one by one they turn to Christ.

These people should not be selected at random, but prayerfully under the guidance of the Spirit. It is likely that they will be drawn from our own families or immediate acquaintances, of our own age, outlook, and sex. Their names should be written (perhaps in code!) and kept carefully in our Bibles, and we should purpose in our hearts to intercede for them every day. Some days we may have great liberty in prayer, but on other occasions we may do little more than name them in God's presence.

Let us remember that although God promises to answer prayer, He never promises to answer this month, this year, or even in this decade! My brother Dick and I more than thirty years ago covenanted to pray for the conversion of a mutual friend, and as I write these lines, this prayer has not yet been answered.

And he gave an illustration to show how necessary it is for people always to pray and never give up. – Luke 18: 1.

From time to time it may be necessary, under the guidance of the Holy Spirit, to revise this list. John, a college student, may be led to pray for the conversion of Charles, his room mate, but after a few years they may drift apart and lose contact with one another, and there may well come a time when John feels that his prayer responsibility for Charles has come to an end, and trusting God to raise up another prayer warrior for Charles, John will, committing his friend finally to God, drop the name off his prayer list.

My wife Jean gives an example of this. She was praying daily for a friend with whom she played golf, a woman with no Christian contacts. After a year she felt her prayer burden lifting, and soon she discovered the reason. "My son went to one of these holy camps last summer," her golfing friend told her, "and what do you think? – he's become a God boy, says he wants to go into the Church," which, by interpretation meant that he had become a Christian, and would now take the responsibility of praying for his mother.

COVENANTED PRAYER

Prayer is never easy, and one of the most difficult aspects of prayer is that of intercession. But this burden is made considerably lighter when it is shared with a partner. Mary did not pray alone for Peter, others shared the task with her – "Prayer was made . . . of the Church . . . for him." Yes, but this agreed partnership in prayer is not only helpful to those who pray, but we must not overlook the fact that the Lord has given a special promise to those who pray in fellowship with others.

> If two of you shall agree on earth as touching anything that they shall ask, it shall be done for them of my Father which is in heaven. For where two or three are gathered together in my name, there am I in the midst of them. – Matthew 18: 19, 20.

Having made a list of people for whose conversion you believe you should pray, with the above promise ringing in your ears, you should next consider enlisting one or more members of your Bible Cell as prayer partners. This again should not be done thoughtlessly, but only after prayerful consideration. Those whom you invite to covenant with you should be spiritually minded folk, in whose judgment and discretion you have complete confidence, and usually those who already know the person for whom you are asking prayer. Don't expect your fellow Christians to give an immediate answer to your request – give them time to think and pray. It may be better to say, "Will you join me in praying daily for the conversion of my brother, John, for the next six months?" rather than "till he turns to Christ". And don't be discouraged if those with heavy prayer commitments have to say 'no'.

The number of those whom you enlist as prayer covenanters should be kept quite small. Always pray and work in strict confidence. Your covenant of prayer must never become widely known, or your strategy might come to the ears of the one for whom you are praying, and that would never do!

For more than ten years following the war, here in Greater London we saw literally hundreds of young men and women (often whole families) turning to Christ, and the reason for this phenomenon was not the efficiency with which the Royal Albert Hall meetings were organised, but because in our summer conferences we inspired and taught Christian people to covenant together in prayer for their non-Christian friends, and the majority of people who came to the Albert Hall meetings were not those who had been invited indiscriminately to join a coach party, but those who had been previously 'softened up' by weeks of covenanted prayer. To encourage your Cell to engage in this type of strategic spiritual warfare, let me give you an example:

PRAY ONE FOR ANOTHER

Margaret, a Christian girl in her mid-twenties, came to a Hildenborough conference where she learned the art of effective witness, personal evangelism, and covenanted intercession. Those with whom she worked in a large city office did not even know that she was a Christian, and she had certainly never won anyone for Christ. But all this was now changed. Her life which had previously been a cul-de-sac, became a through-way for the Lord!

Working at the desk next to Margaret was Joan, an intelligent young woman, who lived in the suburbs with her parents and her brother, Bernard. The four of them were good solid citizens, but completely godless. They neither went to church, prayed, nor read the Bible; indeed, in their home the subject of religion was never mentioned.

Margaret had only been back from her summer holiday two days when it was borne in upon her that here was a girl in deep spiritual need. Guided by the Spirit, Margaret took a card, and on it wrote the name "Joan" (amongst others), and started to concentrate her daily prayers and human friendship upon her workmate. A week or so later Margaret confided in her friend at church, and Margaret and Ruth covenanted together to pray for

Joan's conversion. As the weeks went by, the two girls in the London office seemed more and more drawn to each other, but never once did Margaret talk about her faith – she only prayed for Joan and showed her love and kindness.

One day the following January, as the two girls lunched together, Joan said:

"What are you doing this Saturday night?"

"As a matter of fact, I've got a couple of tickets for the Royal Albert Hall," said Margaret.

"Oh," said Joan, "what is it – a concert?"

Margaret's heart missed a beat! 'Here it comes,' she said to herself.

"No," she replied, sounding as casual as possible. "No, as a matter of fact it's a Christian meeting. I have been to several of them. I find them most inspiring – nearly all young people – huge crowds – and tickets are hard to come by." And then, having started, she just went right ahead and told Joan all about the rallies and about Hildenborough too. It all seemed to come out, and so naturally. Joan was more than slightly interested.

"Do you think you could get me a ticket for one of these Saturdays?" asked Joan.

"Well, it so happens," replied Margaret, "You can have my second ticket this Saturday. Look, why not let's meet for tea at the Marble Arch Corner House at 4.30, and then go along together. The doors open at 6 o'clock."

Joan accepted the invitation with enthusiasm. That night Margaret phoned Ruth and told her the news, and the following evening, Friday, they met and prayed together for Joan.

During the following week it was obvious to Margaret that the rally had made a deep impression on her friend. Joan seemed somewhat subdued, asked several thoughtful questions about the Christian Faith, and suggested that they met and went again together to the next rally. The two prayer partners prayed even more earnestly!

As a result of months of ploughing and harrowing, through Margaret and Ruth's prayers, the soil of Joan's heart and mind was now ready for the good seed of the Word, and the following Saturday, as she sat with thousands of others, she felt as if she was there alone with God. She saw herself as a lost sinner, and better still, she saw Christ crucified and living for her – and in the quiet of her heart she turned to Him in repentance and faith. And during the closing hymn when the speaker asked all those who that night had found new life in Christ to confess Him publicly, she quietly rose to her feet, whilst Margaret, sitting next to her, bowed her head and worshipped, blinking the tears from her eyes.

IF TWO AGREE

For the next few days Joan was lost in wonder, love and praise, but one morning during 'elevenses' she turned to Margaret, and said:

"You know how you told me that you and your friend Ruth teamed up together and prayed for me? Well, I wonder if you would team up with me in praying for my brother, Bernard, and his girl friend, Hilary? Ever since we were kids together Bernard and I have been very near to each other, and Hilary is an absolute dear. And knowing the Lord as I do makes me long that they'll come to know Him too."

That morning another partnership was agreed on earth and registered in Heaven.

During the next twelve months, taught and guided by Margaret, Joan used the same strategy that had been used on her – regular private prayer, no arguing, no nagging, but much Christian love and kindness. Bernard and Hilary were now engaged, and were making final plans for their wedding, and apparently had little interest in anything else. A new series of Saturday youth rallies were just starting in London's Royal Albert Hall, and quite suddenly one day Joan was constrained to invite the young couple to go with her. A little reluctantly, but just to please her, they agreed to go. Joan wrote off at once for the necessary tickets.

Two weeks before the rally, quite unexpectedly Joan was given ten days' holiday 'to start next Friday evening'. She heard the news with mixed feelings. Although she needed a break, she didn't want to jeopardise losing her two 'fish'. However, having extracted a promise from Bernard and Hilary that they would go to the meeting, she went off alone to the West Country for her holiday.

The small Dorset holiday town was very empty, but Joan, now twelve months old in Christ, enjoyed the peaceful atmosphere, and the early spring sunshine. But when Saturday afternoon came, her heart and mind were very much in London, and feeling a deep concern for her brother, after an early tea, she went off again along the cliffs to be alone.

After walking for some while Joan found herself outside a small Norman church, and partly due to a sudden April shower she decided to go in. Closing the heavy oak door behind her she made her way down the aisle, and took her place in the front pew. The silence was broken only by the ticking of the old clock. Glancing at her watch she saw it was ten minutes past six, and as she realised that this was the very moment when Bernard and his fiancée would be arriving at the Royal Albert Hall, she found herself suddenly overwhelmed with a great desire that her brother should come to know the Lord Jesus Whom she herself now loved so deeply. This desire was so great that she dropped to her knees, and poured out her heart in earnest prayer:

"O God," she cried, "hear my prayer for my brother, and give him new Life in Christ this very day."

It had been almost dark when Joan had entered the church, but now as she knelt in prayer, she was conscious of a bright light shining on her. Slowly she opened her eyes – the setting sun had come from behind a dark cloud, and was shining on her face through the ancient stained glass window. As her eyes became accustomed to the light, she saw there, wrought by some medieval craftsman, the figure of Christ standing outside the village of Bethany talking to Martha, and then underneath the picture – it seemed to Joan that He was speaking to her – she read the words "Thy brother shall rise again" (John 11: 23). Then closing her eyes she returned thanks to Him Who once said: "Ask and ye shall receive." As Joan closed the door of the church behind her, the church clock struck 6.30 – the rally was just beginning in the

Thy brother shall rise again

Albert Hall. Joan returned to her hotel walking on air – she need pray no longer. All she could do was to give thanks!

TWO RESERVED SEATS

Soon after Joan had left home for her holiday, a letter reached her from Bernard saying that there were no reserved seats left for the rally, but they planned to arrive before six o'clock and queue up for unreserved seats. This they did, but when they arrived the queue stretched right round the building. They stood in line for nearly half an hour, and then at 6.25, five minutes before the rally was due to start, Bernard turned to Hilary and said:

"It's hopeless, we'll never get in, come on let's go," and they turned to leave; but as they did so, a complete stranger came up and said:

"Would you like two free reserved seats in the stalls – I don't need them."

And so saying, he handed them the tickets and walked away!

Once again, that night, as thousands of Christians all over the country prayed, the power of the Lord was present to heal, and very soon this young couple were leaning forward, listening eagerly to the Word of Life. The address closed with a minute of silent prayer, and in the stillness this young couple passed from death to Life. During the hymn that followed both Bernard and Hilary, at the identical moment, rose to their feet to confess Christ. For one brief moment their eyes met, and then they bowed their heads in prayer.

Soon afterwards yet another prayer partnership was formed consisting of Joan, Bernard and Hilary who covenanted to pray for the conversion of Joan and Bernard's parents.

Today Joan is living in the north of England, and has a wonderful Christian family of her own. Bernard and Hilary's home is like that of Mary the mother of John Mark, whilst Father and Mother, still living in the same house, are both also fully committed Christians.

In recent years many Christian people have come to realise the importance of follow-up after conversion, but thank God, today many are learning often through the Bible Cells, the importance of preparation of heart through covenanted prayer before folk hear the message of life. Reaping is important, but so is ploughing!

WHEN YE PRAY – BELIEVE

But it's high time we returned once again to Mary's Bible Cell

95

which met there in Jerusalem, to learn one more important lesson about prayer – namely, when we pray we must pray in faith. After all, one of the main purposes of prayer is to develop faith, and if we pray without exercising faith, we might just as well not pray at all!

Luke continues the thrilling story by describing Peter's deliverance:

> The same night Peter was sleeping between two soldiers, bound with two chains: and the keepers before the door kept the prison. And, behold, the angel of the Lord came upon him, and a light shined in the prison: and he smote Peter on the side, and raised him up, saying, Arise up quickly. And his chains fell off from his hands. And the angel said unto him, Gird thyself, and bind on thy sandals. And so he did. And he saith unto him, Cast thy garment about thee, and follow me. And he went out, and followed him; and wist not that it was true which was done by the angel; but thought he saw a vision. – Acts 12: 6–9.

Charles Wesley was thinking of this Scripture when he wrote of his own conversion:

> Long my imprisoned spirit lay
> Fast bound in sin and nature's night;
> Thine eye diffused a quickening ray,
> I woke, the dungeon flamed with light:
> My chains fell off, my heart was free;
> I rose, went forth, and followed Thee.

As soon as the Apostle was convinced that his salvation was a fact and not just a vision, he considered what action he should next take:

> And when he had considered the thing, he came to the house of Mary the mother of John, whose surname was Mark; where many were gathered together praying. – Acts 12: 12.

Yes, and when a man is ransomed, healed, restored, forgiven, his first instinct is to join God's people in prayer and thanksgiving. And he went to the house of Mary because he knew that in her home people would be there praying.

THEY WERE ASTONISHED

In that all-night prayer meeting there must have been some very impressive people. Paul and Barnabas were probably there.

A damsel came to hearken, named Rhoda

Some of the other apostles were present, too, with the bishops and elders of the Church in Jerusalem. The prayers were direct and earnest. Each member of the Church was following carefully, ready to join in with a hearty "Amen". But there was one young woman, perhaps only in her teens, who was listening to the prayers with only one ear. Her other ear was open for quite a different sound. She was waiting expectantly to hear the footstep of Simon Peter on the path outside and his familiar knock on the door.

And as Peter knocked at the door of the gate, a damsel came to hearken, named Rhoda. And when she knew Peter's voice, she opened not the gate for gladness, but ran in, and told how Peter stood before the gate. And they said unto her, Thou art mad. But she constantly affirmed that it was even so. Then said they, It is his angel. But Peter continued knocking: and when they had opened the door, and saw him, they were astonished. But he, beckoning unto them with the hand to hold their peace, declared unto them how the Lord had brought him out of the prison. ‑ Acts 12: 13–17.

Can you imagine the expression of consternation on the faces of those church dignitaries and learned brethren when this teenage girl rushed in unannounced, and cried out:

D

"Finish the prayer meeting; get up and sing the doxology. Prayer is answered, Peter is at the door!"

I can imagine, after a sticky silence that could be felt, someone saying: "Rhoda, you are mad," and then a kinder voice, "Rhoda, dear, you will be all right in a minute. You have a touch of religious mania. The all-night prayer meeting has been too much strain for you. Come along, my dear, I will take you outside while the brethren continue with their praying, come along."

"Thank you," said Rhoda, "I am not mad. Have we not been praying for Peter's release?"

"Yes, dear, of course we have, and it's a very nice thought, but come along now."

"Peter is at the door now."

And she constantly affirmed that it was even so. And then they heard Peter's knocking at the door, and as they listened they recognised it as that of their leader, but instead of rejoicing, they looked at one another in horror then someone said:

"It is his angel! He has been beheaded during the night! I knew all along it would happen!"

"But Peter continued knocking," says Luke, "and when they had opened the door, and saw him, they were *astonished*."

"Why! look at this! God has actually answered our prayers! My dear, I do feel bad! I never expected this!"

Then pandemonium broke out till Peter had to beckon to them with his hand to hold their peace.

"Be quiet," he said, "do you want to disturb the whole neighbourhood and have me put back in prison? Where is your faith, your confidence in Christ?"

I believe that Simon Peter was saved from prison and from death, not so much by the prayers of the many who were gathered together praying, but rather by those of the damsel, Rhoda, for she alone was praying with faith, confidently expecting an answer. Remember what Jesus said about prayer?

> I say unto you, What things soever ye desire, when ye pray, believe that ye receive them, and ye shall have them. – Mark 11: 24.

CONFIDENCE IN HIM

When I arose from my knees, having committed my life to Christ, the first thing I had to do was to go to my brother's room and tell him that I had become a Christian. It was the most difficult thing I ever had to do. Only the previous day I was mocking Dick for his faith, and now I thought that either he would be very surprised, or he would not believe that I was telling the truth. But I got the shock, not Dick, for when I told him with much embarrassment that I had just turned to Christ, he looked up at me just as calmly as if I had announced that a meal was ready, and then he said:

"Oh!"

"Yes," I said; "aren't you surprised?"

"No," he said; "not a bit."

"But why aren't you?" I asked.

"Well, you see I have been praying for this, and have been expecting God to answer my prayers any day. I'm not a bit surprised."

The Apostle John, the brother of James and friend of Simon Peter, in the closing paragraph of his first Epistle, says a very beautiful thing which, alas, is usually taken out of its context so that its full significance is lost. I want you to ponder his words:

> And this is the confidence that we have in Him, that, if we ask anything according to His will, He heareth us: And if we know that He hear us, whatsoever we ask, we know that we have the petitions that we desired of Him. If any man see his brother sin . . . he shall ask, and He shall give him life. – 1 John 5: 14–16.

Notice that this wonderful promise applies especially to those of us who are praying for the conversion of others.

1. We must pray with *concentration* – not vaguely, but specifically, concentrating on certain individuals.

2. We must pray with *perseverance* working in partnership with at least one other.

3. We must pray with *faith*, confidently believing that God will hear and answer prayer.

HOLLYWOOD BIBLE CELL

Many Cells were first formed as prayer groups, either to pray for some big evangelistic enterprise, or for some special project in connection with the local church fellowship. The prayer life of a Cell is the best barometer of its spiritual vitality. Little prayer – little vitality; more prayer – more vitality; much prayer – much vitality. Yet in speaking about much prayer I am not thinking primarily of the length of time spent in prayer. Prayer should not be judged by its length, but rather by its intensity. Whilst many Christians pray earnestly before attending an

99

evangelistic meeting, how few ask for God's blessing before going to a Prayer Session? We need to pray that the Holy Spirit will help our infirmities.

O Thou Who camest from above
    The pure celestial fire to impart,
Kindle a flame of sacred love
    On the mean altar of my heart.

There let it for Thy glory burn
With inextinguishable blaze,
And trembling to its source return
    In humble prayer and fervent praise.

One evening I was invited to speak to the Hollywood Christian Group which consists exclusively of people connected with show business. I'll never forget that night. It made a lasting impression on me. My plane was late, and I was driven at a hair-raising speed to an exclusive section in Beverly Hills. I have never seen such a fascinating house – it was built largely of massive plate-glass windows, overlooking a fabulous, sunken swimming pool. I was ushered straight into a vast reception room where more than a hundred most amazing creatures had been waiting for me for more than an hour. I have never seen such an array of such fabulous clothes. I glanced down at my own suit, and felt like a wheelbarrow at the Motor Show! The chairman introduced me briefly, and I got to my feet to speak.

"Flying in I was praying and wondering what I should talk to you about tonight."

I only got as far as this, when a glamorous young woman, who looked about eighteen, sitting right in the front row, looked up at me, and said:

"Doctor Rees, talk to us about prayer – we all want to know how to pray."

Looking down at her I found it hard to believe, with my puritanical Christian views, that she was a Christian at all! Her make-up was so heavy it looked as though she were wearing a mask. Her eyelashes were so long that when she blinked, I expected them to make a swishing noise! What does *she* know about prayer? I asked myself; but of course I had no option, so took the opportunity of telling how my brother Dick covenanted with others and prayed me into the Kingdom, and in this way, without any difficulty, I worked in my testimony of the transforming grace of Christ. Those people listened with rapt attention as for more than half an hour I talked very simply from my own experience of what

I knew of prayer. And then I asked what was no more than a rhetorical question:

"I wonder how many of you know how to pray?"

"Sure," said the girl at my feet, "we know how to pray."

"All right," I said, "let's bow our heads for a prayer now."

I thought that I would lead them myself in a brief prayer, but before our eyes were closed, this girl was pouring out her heart in a simple direct prayer to the Lord, and one after another those people, who to me certainly didn't look like Christians, were talking to God, and it was evident to my mind that to them the Lord Jesus was a living bright reality.

SHORT PRAYERS

Of course we must try to use good language when talking to God, but He is more interested in the desires of our hearts than in the words of our lips.

Once again, whilst visiting various Bible Cells I have been impressed with the infinite variety that there is in how the various Cells pray. Some groups seem to concentrate on simple requests for themselves and one another; others pour out their hearts in confession or thanksgiving to God, but it seems that the majority concentrate on intercession for other people. Some kneel to pray, some stand; whilst others bow their heads reverently as they sit

Pray . . . kneel, stand or sit

in the Presence of the Lord. Some plan in advance for one of their number to lead them in prayer; others pray round in turn; others leave it open to any member of the group to lead; whilst a few spend the time in silent prayer.

Some Cells pray at the outset of their meeting, others at the conclusion; some set aside one meeting in four exclusively for prayer, but to my mind the most effective prayer sessions are those which arise out of the passage which has just been studied (see pages 26 and 54).

It is often said that the family that prays together stays together, and what is true of the family is certainly true of the Bible Cell.

One of the things that I have noted with intense pleasure is that when in Bible Cells they use spoken prayers, the prayers are always brief. I do not know of anything that kills a prayer meeting or a public service like interminable prayers. Jesus taught us that long prayers are heathen, not Christian (Matthew 6: 7). The prayers recorded in the Bible are all brief, with the possible exception of the 119th Psalm, and there the Psalmist prays on the instalment system! At our Hildenborough prayer sessions we have a rule "stand up! speak up! shut up!"

PRAYING ALOUD

It is of the utmost importance that whenever possible each member of the Cell should be encouraged to pray out loud. Just as a newborn babe is encouraged to cry, so the newborn soul should be taught to call God 'my Father' and Jesus Christ 'my Saviour':

> You have been adopted into the very family circle of God and you can say with a full heart, "Father, my Father." –
> Romans 8: 15.

There are certain important milestones in the spiritual experience of a child of God, and these certainly include his conversion, his first confession of Christ, and his first public prayer. I shall not quickly forget the first prayer I prayed in the presence of others. It was painful at the time, but what joy it brought afterwards! Many people find no assurance of new life in Christ until, in the company of others, they pray aloud, naming Christ as their Saviour.

Now how best can we encourage timid people to pray aloud? We must teach them not to ask themselves 'Do I like praying out loud?' but rather 'Would my prayer encourage others, or help those for whom I pray?'; not 'Do I feel led to pray?' but 'Is it my duty to pray?' New Christians should be taught to pray as a mother teaches her child to talk. We should encourage folk to pray briefly. Some people's first prayers are the best prayers: "Lord Jesus, thank you for dying for me, Amen" – "Thank you, O God, for putting it into the hearts of others to pray for me, Amen" – "Please help me at home and at work to witness for Thee, Amen" – "I thank Thee for the Bible, please help me to understand it, Amen" – "Lord, teach me to pray, Amen."

If the members of the Cell are a little nervous, encourage them to write out their prayers in advance, and read them aloud; or to pray one of the Bible prayers, or to select a suitable verse of a hymn and read it out loud (the majority of our hymns are prayers, set to poetry and music).

Some of the most exciting conferences we hold at Hildenborough Hall are those which are run exclusively for newly committed Christians. At one such conference we had more than seventy present, and on the first morning in the chapel, after we had sung a brief hymn, I asked: "How many of you here have ever prayed out loud in the presence of others?" Not more than six hands went up. I then said: "Now I want you to imagine that you are going to be granted an Audience with the Lord Himself, and that He is going to grant you just one request, anything you wish to ask. Now what will be your request? Let's close our eyes for a moment and each think of the answer." After a few moment's silence, I continued:

"Now, let's start here at the front and go round everybody, and I want each of you to tell us what it was that you decided to ask." Everyone without exception spoke up: "That my whole family may become Christians," "That God will send peace throughout the world," "That God will bless all the missionaries." . . . .

"Now," I said, "We are going round again in the same order, and I want each one of you to repeat again exactly what you said just now, with this difference. We shall have our eyes closed, and instead of your talking to us, I want you to talk to God. Start off 'O Lord' and then repeat what you said just now, and close with an 'Amen'." And off they went. The first one said, "O Lord, may all my family soon become Christians, Amen" – "O Lord, please send peace throughout the world, Amen" – "O Lord, please bless all the missionaries, Amen." Everyone took part. I then said: "Now how many of you have taken part in prayer out loud for the first time this morning?" Naturally, nearly seventy hands went up, and you should have seen the joy reflected in those eager faces!

One of the things that prevents people taking part in an open prayer session is the fear that someone else will start at precisely the same moment. The best way of overcoming this problem is by passing a Bible or hymn book round, the leader first explaining: "Now, we are going to pass my Bible round the group, and who- ever is holding the Bible will be free to take part in a brief prayer. Remember, you must only pray aloud if you are holding the Bible. If, when the Bible comes to you, you do not wish to take part, don't be embarrassed, just pass it on to the next person." This simple method has encouraged not only young people, but adults to pray aloud. But whatever happens, never get into a rut. A rut is a grave with the ends knocked out!

Sometimes, if the members of your Cell know each other well, it might be a good idea for them to pray round for one another. Say there are twelve people sitting in a circle, let the leader suggest that first no. 1 prays by name for no. 12, then no. 2 prays for no. 1, and no. 3 for no. 2, and so on round the circle.

Many helpful sermons have been preached and books written on the subject of prayer, but after all the only way to learn how to pray, is to pray, and when men and women get together and expose themselves to God by praying together, miracles are bound to take place. Lord, teach us to pray!

A Bible Cell leader should do his utmost to encourage each member to pray aloud; but at all costs he should avoid embarrass- ing them so that they are too scared to come again. There are some folk who are far too shy or self-conscious ever to take part.

A bruised reed shall he not break, and smoking flax shall he not quench. – Matthew 12: 20.

I have written fully about Bible Study and Prayer, which are the first two common characteristics of Bible Cells, and now, by way of contrast, a very brief word on the third, which is Fellowship.

III. FELLOWSHIP

Mr. and Mrs. Donaldson, who live just outside London, have for many years spent all their spare time playing Bridge and attending gay parties, never giving God a thought. Two or three years ago a Bible Cell was formed in their area, and a Christian couple attending the Cell won the confidence of Mr. and Mrs. Donaldson through the common interest that they had in gardening. After some weeks of preparation, by persistent, covenanted prayer, the Donaldsons accepted an invitation to attend a coffee evening arranged by the group, and soon they found themselves deeply interested in the things of God, and by and by they both passed from death to Life.

"The thing that amazes us," Mr. Donaldson told me, "is the warm fellowship of Christian people. The Masons have nothing to touch it. Indeed, the ties that bind Christian people together seem to be stronger than those of blood relationship."

The Apostle John was obviously a most affectionate man, and he explains the secret of Christian love this way:

> Every one that loveth him that begat loveth him also that is begotten of him – 1 John 5: 1.

The strength of the 18th-century Evangelical awakening was in the innumerable class meetings (Bible Cells) which sprang up everywhere. It has often been pointed out that no one since John Wesley has been able to reach the British working man with the Gospel. His secret was to be found in the warm fellowship which these neglected men found in the early Methodist class meetings. Alas! today our formal religious services only repel these needy men, and drive them to the comradeship of the communist cell. The warm Christian fellowship found in Bible Cells throughout the world is something which cannot be described in words. It has to be experienced to be understood.

Next we will turn our attention to Evangelism, which is the fourth of the five common characteristics of Bible Cells.

IV. EVANGELISM

Paul ends his Letter to the Christians in Ephesus with a stirring word of exhortation, commencing with the sentence:

> Wherefore take unto you the whole armour of God, that ye may be able to withstand in the evil day, and having done all, to stand. – Ephesians 6: 13 ff.

The Apostle then names the seven pieces of armour which go to make up the panoply of God. The first five pieces which he names are all defensive weapons. (1) the girdle of truth, (2) the breastplate of righteousness, (3) the shoes of the preparation of the gospel, (4) the shield of faith, (5) the helmet of salvation; but notice that the last two weapons that he describes, pieces 6 and 7, are both offensive weapons. The first five are entrusted to the Christian soldier to defend him from the fiery darts of the wicked, but the last two that he might drive the enemy back, and these latter are:

(6) *the sword of the Spirit – the Word of God*
And take . . . the sword of the Spirit, which is the Word of God. – Ephesians 6: 17.

(7) *the Power of the Spirit – persevering prayer*
praying always with all prayer and supplication in the Spirit, and watching thereunto with all perseverance and supplication for all saints. – Ephesians 6: 18.

We speak in awe of the power of atomic weapons, but men's weapons are feeble when compared with the mighty arsenal which the Church of Jesus Christ has at its disposal in the Bible and Prayer.

These two deadly weapons are only fully effective when used together. In battle, what use is a sharp, two-edged sword if there is no skilful, mighty hand to wield it? And what is the use of a skilful, mighty hand if there is no sword to wield? It is through His Word that God gives us the Gospel we preach. It is through effective prayer that God gives us the power with which to preach and teach His Word. Preaching is talking to men about God; praying is talking to God about men. If, therefore, in our preaching we are to prevail with men for God, first in our praying we must prevail with God for men.

Just as in the animal world it takes male and female to reproduce life, so in the spiritual realm, it takes the Word of God and prayer; the Gospel and the power of the Holy Spirit to produce Divine Life.

EZEKIEL'S VISION

Ezekiel's vision (Ezekiel 37: 1 ff.) reminds us forcibly of this principle. The bones which the prophet saw in the open valley were very many, and very dry, and they presented a challenge to his faith:

And he said unto me, Son of man, can these bones live?
And I answered, O Lord God, thou knowest. – Ezekiel 37: 3.

And how were those dry bones transformed into an exceeding

great army? By the Word of God and the Spirit of God; by preaching and praying.

Again he said unto me prophesy (preach) upon these bones, and say unto them O ye dry bones, hear the Word of the Lord. Thus saith the Lord God unto these bones; Behold, I will cause breath to enter into you, and ye shall live. And I will lay sinews upon you, and will bring up flesh upon you, and cover you with skin, and put breath in you, and ye shall live; and ye shall know that I am the Lord. So I prophesied (preached) as I was commanded: and as I prophesied (preached), there was a noise, and behold a shaking, and the bones came together, bone to his bone. – Ezekiel 37: 4–7.

Ezekiel's preaching was orthodox and Biblical, but all it did was to add sinews, flesh and skin to the dead bones. Orthodox preaching and witnessing, important as it is, is simply not enough. God spoke again to the prophet:

Prophesy unto the wind, prophesy, son of man, and say to the wind, Thus saith the Lord God; Come from the four winds, O breath, and breathe upon these slain, that they may live. – Ezekiel 37: 9.

Notice first, he preached, he talked to the dry bones about God, and then he prayed, he talked to God about the dry bones. It was not his orthodox preaching alone, nor his earnest intercession alone. It was the combination of both; it was the joint operation of the Word of the Lord and the Wind (Spirit or Breath) of the Lord which produced new life.

Our Lord referred to these two weapons when He said:

Ye do err, not knowing the Scriptures, nor the Power of God. – Matthew 22: 29.

OUTREACH

We have been considering the vital ministry of effective prayer, both by the individual member and entire Bible Cell, and its importance cannot be over emphasized; but at the same time each disciple and each Cell must bear in mind that they have a duty not only to pray and intercede to God, but also to preach and bear witness to those for whom they pray.

A Bible Cell exists not as a mutual admiration society, nor merely as a class for Bible Study, but to make Christ known to men and women in the Community. A Cell is not an end in itself, but a means to an end.

There are many varied methods of communicating the good news of Christ to our contemporaries, but I have noticed that Bible Cells concentrate largely upon the following seven methods. Let me name the methods, and then say a word about each.

1. Personal Witness and Evangelism
2. Guest Bible Studies
3. Guest Coffee Mornings/Evenings
4. Guest Luncheon/Dinner Parties
5. Houseparties
6. Public Lectures
7. Public Bible Expositions

1. Personal Evangelism

Members of every lively Bible Cell are constantly encouraging, inspiring, and teaching one another to win others for Christ by personal evangelism. Some Cells arrange special courses of Bible Study on the subject; others pray and discuss together how best they can bear witness in their daily lives. One Cell, having completed a course of studies on personal work, decided that during the following week each member would seek to lead someone to Christ, and at their next meeting report on their experiences. (Passages from John's Gospel, dealing with Personal Evangelism, are given on page 84.)

There are many helpful books and booklets available on witnessing and personal evangelism,* some of which are suitable for group study.

An experienced soul winner can do a tremendous lot of useful work in a Bible Cell if he will tell others of his experiences in personal witnessing. In spite of modern methods, I am still a firm believer in learning by the old apprenticeship method. This is how the Master trained and taught His Apostles, taking them along with Him to listen to what He preached, and to watch His technique.

In every method of communicating the Gospel, we must bear in mind that God is not concerned only with quantity, but quality. There is no easy method of winning souls. When I first became a Christian I would spend a vast amount of time and energy putting

* Send stamped addressed envelope to The Bookroom, Hildenborough Hall, Otford Hills, Sevenoaks, Kent, England, for full particulars of these books and booklets.

Gospels through letter boxes, and standing in the market place distributing tracts as if I were advertising a new detergent! It may be that God still guides some of His servants into this sort of activity, but many years ago I learnt that usually to witness effectively I must first prepare a man's heart by prayer, then by showing him love and friendship, win his confidence, and earn the right to speak to him about the Lord Jesus.

Members of the Cell should constantly share with one another their experiences in personal witnessing, their failures and triumphs, each seeking both to learn and to teach.

Just after I became a Christian, Sister Stubbings of The Church Army gave me a book which she told me had been a blessing to her when, as a young woman, she was converted to Christ through hearing Dr. R. A. Torrey preaching in the Guildhall, Cambridge. The book was entitled *How to bring Men to Christ* by R. A. Torrey (still available in the U.S.A.). I read this book in the train travelling to and from London, at the same time looking up the references in my Bible. This book brought me assurance of life and the know-how of soul winning.

2. Guest Bible Studies

I have lost count of the times I have heard of non-Christian people attending verse-by-verse Bible Studies, and sitting with the Word of God in their hand, have seen the Way of Life and turned to the Lord. Many still believe that if the sinner is going to turn to Christ, he must do so in an evangelistic meeting, and that the Bible Study is reserved exclusively for enlightened Christians; but it seems that God's Spirit delights to work in ways far removed from the preconceived ideas of His people. One of the many exciting things about this Bible Cell movement is that non-Christians are finding new life in Christ whilst sitting in a neighbour's home, reading and studying the Bible. Many of our contemporaries are not prepared to go to Church, or a crusade to listen to an evangelistic sermon, but many, if approached in the right way, are more than willing to attend an informal Bible Study in which they themselves can participate by asking questions and making suggestions. This is largely due to modern methods of education. Many of us are far too conservative in our methods of evangelism; we must be on our toes to exploit this situation for God.

Sometimes I am tempted to think that the Word of our Lord spoken in His day to the Pharisees might also be addressed to those of us who today call ourselves Bible Christians:

Ye have made the commandment of God of none effect by your tradition. – Matthew 15: 6.

Now our traditions tell us that if a man has not yet embraced salvation through faith in Christ, his religion, Bible reading, prayers, self-denial, generosity, honesty, and good works count for nothing. Indeed, I have often heard evangelists say: "You go to church, you read your Bible, you say your prayers, you do good works, you keep the commandments. What's the good of that? None of those things, nor all of those things will ever save you."

Now, whereas this statement is true, it is also at the same time very misleading. In recent years God has taught me that we should do all we can to persuade our non-Christian friends to go to church, to read and study the Bible, to pray about their daily problems, and to endeavour to keep God's law, for while it is perfectly true that no man can merit salvation by attending church, reading the Bible, saying prayers, and keeping the commandments, it is also true that the non-Christian man who goes to church regularly, and hears the Gospel is far more likely to find salvation through faith in Christ than the man who goes nowhere except to the cinema. The non-Christian man who, daily and thoughtfully, searches and reads the Bible is far more likely to find God in Christ than the man who reads nothing but the *Daily Mirror* and the *News of the World*. The non-Christian man who, every morning, kneels and prays to God for light and direction, is far more likely to find God than the man who lives like an animal as if he had no soul at all. The non-Christian man who sincerely seeks to keep the commandments, even though he fails, is far more likely to find new life in Christ than the man who flings all moral restraint to the wind.

We must not only encourage non-Christians to attend the evangelistic meeting, but also the evangelical Church; to read the Bible, to pray, to keep the commandments, because it is through these avenues, God's people, the Scriptures, Prayer, and the Law that God approaches men. In church we hear the Bible read and the Gospel preached. In the Bible we are brought face to face with Christ. In prayer we open our souls to the influence of the Holy Spirit. In endeavouring to keep the commandments, we discover our own sinfulness and thus the Law is a schoolmaster to bring us to Christ.

CORNELIUS

God taught me a great deal some years ago through a careful study of Acts chapter 10. Cornelius, an army officer with the 2nd

Italian Cohort of Roman citizens was devout, religious, earnest, God-fearing, prayerful, self-denying, just, blameless, and held in good report, but in spite of this, he was obviously lacking salvation – he was lost.

> Call for Simon, whose surname is Peter; who shall tell thee words, whereby thou and all thy house shall be saved. – Acts 11: 13, 14.

Yet, nevertheless, God both heard his prayers, and was mindful of his almsgiving and good works.

> And he (the angel) said unto him (Cornelius) Thy prayers and thine alms are come up for a memorial before God. – Acts 10: 4.

Is that mother you are prayerfully seeking to win for Christ distressed about her sick child in hospital? Is that business man whose name is on your prayer list burdened about staff or financial problems? Or, has that youth in the factory just lost his mother? Then please, please *don't* say: "It's no use your praying about these things, God is not interested in the prayer of lost people." No, a thousand times, no. Surely *this* is the Master's way: "You have my deepest sympathy. How I wish I could do something to help! I remember how I felt when a similar thing happened to me. But I wonder if I might make a suggestion? As you know, I believe in prayer. How would it be if we both agreed to make this problem of yours a real matter of prayer. I'll kneel tonight and pray for you, if you will promise to do the same." Scores of godless, worldly men and women in recent years have made their first move towards God in a situation like this. Once they have started to pray, the next step is to suggest they start reading the Bible or attending a Bible Study, then as God guides you, invite them to come to Christ. I can hear someone say: "Yes, I've tried all that, but it didn't work!" But perhaps it failed for this very reason – *you* tried it! This is not our work – it is the work of God's Spirit. Our part is simply to obey and trust God, to pray and bear witness – the miracles we must leave to Him.

> Fear ye not, stand still, and see the salvation of the Lord, which he will shew to you today: for the Egyptians whom ye have seen today, ye shall see them again no more for ever. The Lord shall fight for you, and ye shall hold your peace. – Exodus 14: 13, 14.

I have already given you an example as to how God works in

converting people to Himself in Bible Cells, in telling you the story of the conversion of Charles and Ruth Tedder, so I will not burden you with further examples here. However, I should like to share with you some of the things that I have learnt recently in this particular method of evangelism.

A non-Christian person should not be invited to attend a Bible Study:

(*a*) unless much prayer has been made for him previously;

(*b*) unless the whole Cell are unanimous that he should be invited;

(*c*) unless he is a man who, by his presence, will not spoil the work of God's Spirit in the study of His Word. It would not, for instance, be wise to invite an aggressive atheist, humanist, or unitarian to the group. He should be a man who is either consciously seeking Christ or who is teachable, in that he has an open mind;

(*d*) as a permanent member of the group, but merely for one or two weeks, to see whether or not he finds it helpful. When he comes, he should be introduced to each member of the Cell, and made thoroughly at home.

Some Bible Cells, very wisely, from time to time plan special Guest Bible Studies, and they will select some passage such as "Naaman, the Leper" which Mr. Thornton used when Charles and Ruth Tedder came. If some of their guests are bored, then they need not be asked again, but if others seem deeply interested, and want to hear more, then these folk can be invited to come again to further studies.

An enthusiastic member of a Bible Cell who goes out beseeching all and sundry to attend, will most certainly wreck the work of a Cell, perhaps beyond repair.

When unconverted men come into a friendly home and sit down with a group of lively Christian people, and expose themselves to the Word of God, miracles are bound to take place, but it is God Who works the miracles. He doesn't ask *us* to work miracles; He merely invites us to go along with Him, and watch Him at work. Peter, James, and John saw the Master working miracles that no one else saw, simply because they lived much nearer to Him. When a Cell of Christian people walk closely with their Lord through prayer, the Word of God, faith, and obedience, they too will see the same Lord at work.

Welcome!

MAKING THEM AT HOME

Now here I must say something which is of the utmost importance. Indeed, I feel so strongly about it that I would like it to be printed in large letters at the top of every page of this book! It is about our attitude of mind towards the non-Christian who may attend our Bible Cell, either as an occasional visitor, or as a regular Bible student.

Either the group will be told in advance by the member who is bringing the guest that the newcomer is not yet an enlightened Christian, or the fact will very soon become apparent; but whatever happens – and this is the important thing – the newcomer must be made to feel really welcome. We must at all costs avoid the 'we are holier than thou' attitude in our conversation and prayers. In no circumstances must we imply, 'You know nothing – we have all the answers,' 'You're lost – we're saved,' 'You're in the darkness – we're in the light.' Nor must we ever pray aloud, "And Lord, if there should be one in our midst who doesn't yet know Thee. . . ." If the non-Christian guest is welcomed with genuine love and friendship, and is surrounded by our prayers, as he sits with an open Bible, the Holy Spirit Himself will soon make him conscious of the Presence of God, revealing to him his sin and the way of new life through Christ. This is the work of the Holy Spirit which He can best accomplish without our tactless prodding.

If at a full church meeting you are all speaking with tongues and men come in who are both uninstructed and without faith, will they not say that you are insane? But if you are preaching God's Word and such a man should come in to your meeting, he is convicted and challenged by your united speaking of the truth. His secrets are exposed and he will fall on his knees acknowledging God and saying that God is truly among you! – I Corinthians 14: 23–25.

No, let our attitude of mind be humble and honest when the non-Christian visitor attends our Cell.

"Tonight we have a special welcome for John McKnight who is here as the guest of Harry and Jane. John, we want you to know how glad we are to have you, and we want you to feel at home. Let me assure you that we are not experts. We are all learning together, and we feel sure that your presence will help us. No doubt Harry and Jane will have told you how we study together. We hope you'll enjoy yourself. Please don't hesitate to join in even if it's only by asking a question. I am sure I shan't know the answer, but maybe together as a group we'll come up with something that may help. We're planning to have a short time of general prayer at the close of our study, and if you would like to join in, by all means do. If, on the other hand, you would rather listen to others, don't feel you have let the group down in any way."

There may be some who regard this approach with suspicion, but surely honesty is the best policy, particularly in spiritual things. No man who knows anything about the Bible imagines that he knows all the answers. The difference between the profound Bible student and the novice is that one has conscious ignorance, and the other unconscious ignorance.

A minister, or evangelist, preaching from a public pulpit can, and should be intensely personal, but in Bible Cell evangelism we must take great care not to lay the snare in the sight of the bird. Each new guest must be welcomed as a friend and a fellow student.

One of the many great advantages of winning people to Christ actually in the Bible Cell meeting, is that follow-up is automatically taken care of in the life and fellowship of the Cell.

3. Guest Coffee Mornings/Evenings

A very large proportion of the Cells plan regular or occasional Coffee Mornings or Guest Evenings to which the members, after much prayer, invite their non-Christian friends and neighbours. These informal Coffee Meetings take many varied forms. Sometimes they are held in the same home, and at the same time as the normal meeting of the Cell; sometimes they are held in a home – Christian or non-Christian – which is able to accommodate a greater number. Quite often they are held in a café or hotel lounge. They are never advertised widely. Usually special invitation cards are printed. A copy of one such card lies in front of me as I write:

....

Request the pleasure of the company of

Mr. & Mrs....................................

to

An Informal Coffee Evening in the home of:
Mr. & Mrs. Paul Gates,
"Onnalea", Bantham,
at 7.00 p.m. on Saturday, October 26
To meet Mr. Tom Rees who will speak on the subject
I WAS AN AGNOSTIC
Questions and Discussion

R.S.V.P.

Here are some titles which have been used recently:

An Astronomer	– 'Has this Planet been visited?'
An Archaeologist	– 'Does Archaeology confirm the Bible?'
A successful Business Man	– 'I was an Alcoholic.'
A Christian Author	– 'How I Write my Books.'
A Child Psychologist	– 'Teaching the Christian Faith to Children.'
A Borstal Institution Teacher	– 'Juvenile Delinquency – Its Cause and Its Cure.'
A Christian Doctor	– 'Why do Young People take Drugs?'
A Professor of Chemistry	– 'Science or Religion – Do we have to Choose?'
A Christian Lawyer	– 'Can Intelligent People believe in the Resurrection?'
A Christian J.P.	– 'Christianity – Revelation or Speculation?'
A Professor of Law	– 'Is Christianity Unique?'
A well-known Scientist	– 'Has Science outmoded Christianity?'
A well-known Cricketer	– 'Scoring for Jesus Christ.'

When arranging such an evening, do not fall into the common error of imagining that success can only be gauged by the numbers who attend, or by those who profess to turn to Christ. In the work of God numbers are not important. A sense of God's Presence *is* important. Outward professions matter very little; inward conviction *is* all important.

Great care should be taken to see that these occasions do not deteriorate into a happy night out for Christian people. It has been my privilege to be the speaker at many of these coffee meetings, and I am always delighted to be told in advance: "Christian people will not be permitted to attend unless they bring with them at least one person who, as far as they know, is not yet a committed Christian." Obviously, before the meeting takes place, the Cell will hold special prayer sessions where, in the strictest confidence, they will perhaps pray for their 'fish' by name. Refreshments are usually served at the beginning whilst people are coming in. The refreshments should be as simple as possible. Singing, an opening prayer, or a Bible reading are invariably considered out of place. The appointed host or chairman should, in a sentence, welcome the people, introduce the guest speaker and his subject, thank him for coming, and tell the company that after the talk the speaker will be glad to answer questions. Naturally, during his address the speaker will either read or quote the Bible, and will probably conclude with a brief prayer.

The speaker must be able to communicate the Christian message in language his hearers will readily understand. If the guests are mostly church-goers, then of course he can use the 17th-century language of the Authorised Version. If, on the other hand, they are ignorant of the Bible and theological terms, then he will not talk of the 'Incarnation', but of the Birth of Christ; not of 'Justification', but of Forgiveness or Acquittal; not of 'Conversion', but of turning to Christ; not of 'Regeneration', but of new Life; not of 'Redemption', but of being bought back.

It's not only the guest speaker, but every Cell member who needs to learn how to express the Christian message in terms that the uninitiated can readily grasp. The Rev. John Wesley was a brilliant linguist. He corresponded with his family in Latin. He was a good Greek Scholar, and well acquainted with the Hebrew tongue. Moreover, he spoke and wrote several modern languages fluently. Yet, when he started preaching in English to the common people of his day, he discovered that his hearers just didn't understand his language, so Wesley had to learn yet another entirely new language – the language of the common man. Calling an illiterate servant girl into his study, he said:

"Now Mary, I want you to listen carefully to me. I am going to read one of my sermons to you, and each time I use a word or a phrase you do not fully understand, you are to stop me."

So, with the help of Mary he learned a new language, and went forth in the power of the Holy Spirit to offer Christ freely to the people of England in the tongue they spoke and understood.

The message of the Gospel is always the same, but human language is constantly changing, and the personal witness and public speaker, to be effective, must learn to speak in terms that people understand.

Some people believe that all we have to do is to expound the Bible, and if we are addressing people who are acquainted with the Bible and its technical terms, then we can safely do just that, but alas, the majority of our contemporaries know little of the Bible, and still less of theological terms.

As I pointed out before, when the Apostle Peter preached the Gospel to Bible-loving Jews on the Day of Pentecost, he did very little more than quote large passages from the Old Testament (Acts 2), but when preaching the same message to Captain Cornelius and his fellow army officers, he didn't quote one word of the Bible (Acts 10).

4. Guest Luncheon and Dinner Parties

The idea of evangelistic luncheon and dinner parties is as old as the New Testament itself. As we have already pointed out, it was probably the Master Himself Who suggested to Matthew, Zacchaeus and others that following their conversion they should invite their neighbours to dinner in order that He might present His message, and that they might give their witness.

In the U.S.A. Men's Breakfast Groups have been used to the conversion of countless business and professional men. The Christian Women's Clubs of America have been growing for more than twenty-seven years, and these women have demonstrated how carefully planned luncheons and dinners, backed up by prayer, are a most effective method of reaching non-Christians with the Word of Life.

Once again the form of these Christian luncheons and dinners varies tremendously. Usually they are held in a suitable hotel or restaurant, though sometimes a non-Christian couple are asked if they will lend their house for the occasion, when the members of the Cell will prepare a buffet luncheon or supper. Once again the speaker and his subject must be chosen with much care. Sometimes the group themselves will be responsible for the finances, although

All things to all men, that I might by all means save some

usually when the function is held in an hotel or restaurant, members of the Cell will pay for their own meals and that of their guests. Invitations are attractively printed, including the note 'Tickets 17/6d. each'. In other words, each guest pays for his own meal.

The Christian Lunch and Dinner Clubs sometimes have a special feature as well as a guest speaker, such as floral decoration, hat making, cooking demonstration, etc. A host and hostess and chairman should always be appointed. Be sure to arrange with the caterers in advance that as soon as coffee is served, the waiters vacate the dining-room so that there is no movement or distraction during the talk. The chairman should once again welcome the guests, introduce and thank the guest speaker, and all this should be done in a maximum time of three minutes.

Recently I was invited to address nearly 400 men at one of these dinner parties in Canada. Towards the end of the meal the chairman turned to me with a look of horror on his face – "Oh dear," he said, "Just look what's happening. These men are lighting up cigarettes. Whatever shall I say?" I looked at him with a big smile, and said "Do nothing – just thank God, and pray.

I'd rather see the men taking cigarettes from their pockets than Bibles, for this is a sign that we have the men we are after."

Obviously not every Bible Cell will be able to arrange evangelistic luncheon and dinner parties. Jesus asked rich men like Matthew and Zacchaeus to put on parties for Him because they had large homes and plenty of domestic help. The Master did not even suggest a coffee morning to the blind beggar Bartimaeus.

5. Houseparties

In seeking to win men and women for Christ I have used all kinds of buildings – town halls, churches, cinemas, chapels, theatres, mission halls, dance halls, and the open air, but after many years of experience I do not hesitate to say that a home presents the best venue and atmosphere in which to tell the good news. This is partly due to the fact that in a home people do not feel that they have to be on their best behaviour. In most homes there is a relaxed and happy atmosphere in which even the most critical unconsciously let down their defences. It has been wisely said Christianity is not only taught, but caught. Don't misunderstand me, no one believes more than I do in teaching the Christian faith, but if as we teach the truth there is not that indescribable sense of His Power and His Presence, then our teaching will be in vain. When our Lord preached the Word of God, we are told that the Power of the Lord was present to heal.

> And it came to pass on a certain day, as he was teaching . . .
> the power of the Lord was present to heal them. – Luke
> 5: 17.

Immediately after we were married, my wife, Jean, and I knelt in the lounge of our new home, and we dedicated it to God, telling Him that it would be always open to His people, and to those who were in need. During the first twelve months seldom a day passed without someone coming in for a midday meal or evening meal, and quite often for breakfast. Moreover, our visitors' book for that year shows that our spare room was occupied on nearly 365 nights, so next time we moved, we took a house with seven bedrooms and the same thing happened there, and we quickly learned that open hearts and open homes are the best way of taking men alive, and in 1938, just before the war broke out, we decided that we would look for a really large house which we could use as a home base for evangelism, and this is how Hildenborough Hall was started.

Since we opened in November 1945 we have entertained considerably more than 80,000 in our houseparties. We thank God that today there are literally thousands of men and women scattered all over the world serving God as doctors, nurses, teachers, missionaries, and ministers, who first met the Master in our home.

I have asked hundreds of newly committed disciples the question:

"What exactly was it that made you turn to Christ?" They may use different words, but again and again they come up with the same answer:

"I can't tell you exactly what it was, but as soon as I came in it was here."

"Would you say," I ask, "that it is a sense of the Presence of the Lord Himself?"

"Yes, that's it. He was here. I felt His Presence as soon as I entered the house, and I seem to see Him in the other guests, and in the Christian staff."

Our task, therefore, is not merely to teach people the truth, but to bring them into a living Christian fellowship where they will be conscious of the Power and Presence of the Lord Himself. And a company of Christians who are living together in love and fellowship produces just this sense of His Presence.

When I went to the Parish church, Sevenoaks, in 1930 to take charge of the work amongst the young people, I found that my preaching to them did little or no good. It wasn't until I took the boys away to camp for a couple of weeks, appointing keen Christian officers, that they started to turn to Christ.

Throughout the 1930s each summer I took large parties of boys from the East End of London into the heart of the country camping. Yes, I visited them in their homes, but it wasn't until they were conscious of the Power and Presence of Christ in a Christian community that they turned to the Saviour.

Several times each year we arrange special Weekend House-parties at Hildenborough Hall. These do not appear on our prospectus, nor are they advertised in any way. Some are for senior teenagers, others for young adults in the 20–35 age bracket, and some are for couples over 35. We have a number of dedicated Christian friends in these three age brackets, and with them we pray and plan each detail. The Christian folk are only permitted to come if they bring with them at least one non-Christian guest for whose conversion they are praying. What amazing miracles we have seen!

Many evangelical churches have discovered the inestimable value of a weekend houseparty or retreat. A year or so ago an

120

evangelical minister filled two large coaches with the members of his church, and brought them to Hildenborough for a weekend. I met that man again some twelve months later, and he told me:

"That weekend did more for the spiritual life of my church than all my twelve years of preaching put together."

Bible Cells in this country and overseas are reaping a tremendous spiritual harvest by using the houseparty method of introducing others to Christ. All across the American continent there are innumerable Christian Guest Houses and Conference Centres which are available for this purpose, and I am glad to say that since the end of the war many have been opened up in Great Britain. An individual Cell, or two or three combining together could, with very little difficulty, take a sizeable party of carefully invited guests away for a weekend retreat or houseparty. The plans must be carefully worked out approximately twelve months in advance. Every detail must be covered by prayer. A simple brochure should be drawn up and either printed or duplicated. It should be made clear that the houseparty is 'by special invitation only'. Normally it is better to segregate the ages as suggested before. A host and hostess, or a guest speaker should be invited to lead the informal talks and sessions. It should be made clear on the folder that there will be ample time for rest and recreation. At the same time the object of the weekend must also be set out clearly.

Hildenborough Hall, Otford Hills, Sevenoaks, Kent
GUEST WEEKEND HOUSEPARTY
Friday, January 31 – Monday, February 3

Host and Hostess

....

Special Guests

....

....

....

This Houseparty is being planned by the members of The Hildenborough Senior Council as a quiet and restful retreat high up on the North Downs in the Garden of England. Guests will have an opportunity of thinking and talking together over the relevance of Christian Faith and Ethics in the contemporary scene. There will be informal talks, discussions and question sessions on the place of Christianity in personal, family, business, and national life. The aim of this party is to help one another in our problems, seeking the inspiration and guidance of God. There will be ample opportunity for rest and relaxation.

Some Bible Cell members are able and willing to pay for the guests whom they invite, but usually, provided plenty of notice is given, people are only too happy to pay their own expenses for the weekend. The sessions at these houseparties should be kept extremely informal, giving the guests ample opportunity to participate in the discussions, and to ask questions. Such an enterprise, if guided by God and blessed by His Spirit, will not only result in the true conversion of men and women to Christ, but in untold spiritual blessing in the life of the Bible Cell.

6. Public Lectures

Another method of evangelism widely used amongst the Bible Cells is that of arranging public lectures in a large hall or hotel ballroom. These are either a series of six or eight monthly lectures, or individual lectures arranged from time to time.

With the co-operation of various Bible Cells throughout London and the Home Counties we recently held such a series in the London Hilton Hotel, Park Lane, under the title 'The Christian Faith in a Contemporary World'. Professor Robert Boyd spoke on 'Has this Planet been Visited?' John Stott on 'What is Man?' John Taylor, on 'Does Archaeology Confirm the Bible?' We also organised another series of lectures in the Royal Festival Hall for Fifth and Sixth Formers under the general title 'Science and Religion'. Well-known Christian professors and experts covered such subjects as 'Science or Religion – Do we have to Choose?', 'Does the Creation story Conflict with Modern Science?', 'Can Science explain the Nature of Man?' 'Has Science outmoded Christianity?'

Whereas the houseparty is always informal, the lectures are far more formal. All you need is a good chairman who, in a business-like way, will make the announcements of forthcoming lectures, introduce and thank the lecturer, and then tell the audience that at the conclusion they may address their questions direct to the speaker. If refreshments can be available at the close, it does make it a great deal easier for personal contact. In planning these lectures it should be borne in mind that the object is to present the Christian Gospel in such a way that men and women who hear will turn to the Lord in repentance and living faith. Our object is not to entertain, nor merely to teach, but to convert sinners to Christ. Alas, there are many places where a plain statement of the Christian Gospel is seldom, if ever, heard.

7. Public Bible Expositions

Home Bible Study Groups inevitably create a desire for further instruction in the Scriptures, and for this reason ministers who faithfully expound the Word of God find that through the use of Bible Cells their Sunday Church congregations are greatly increased in numbers. But alas such ministers are not to be found in every area, but throughout this country, and overseas too, it is thrilling to see how the Holy Spirit is guiding His people in the Bible Cells to arrange regular public expositions of Scripture.

A central church lends itself admirably to such work, and usually the minister and his church officers are only too willing for the building to be used, provided, of course, the out-of-pocket expenses of lighting, heating, and cleaning are taken care of. When a church is used, it is sometimes important that in the printing, under the name of the church, it should be stated "Used by kind permission", otherwise local people might think that it was organised only by the members of that particular church.

Often the same expositor is invited to come for six or eight consecutive months. This gives him an opportunity to tackle a series of Bible Readings, but on other occasions it is felt to be better to have a different expositor each month. The speaker again must be chosen with the utmost care under the guidance of the Holy Spirit. Thank God in this country, and in the United States, there are many gifted ministers and laymen who are well able to present an instructive, challenging exposition. The speaker should be asked to keep the evangelistic note well to the fore, and to bear in mind that there will be many non-Christians and spiritual babes present. Mr. Spurgeon's advice might not be out of place: "Please remember – be simple. Don't preach over people's heads. Our Lord said 'feed my sheep' not my giraffes!"

The pattern of these expositions varies from place to place. Usually the chairman announces a well-known hymn, and calls upon a local minister or Christian leader to pray. The chairman then makes the announcements, introducing the guest speaker, and hands over the rest of the hour to him.

Sometimes the organisers prefer to take care of the expenses themselves, but the usual custom is to take up a straightforward collection to cover the cost of the rent of the hall, advertising, and the speaker's travelling expenses.

Talking of speaker's expenses, remember that if your speaker is a full-time minister of a church, a professional or business man, then all you need do is to pay his out-of-pocket travelling expenses. No – don't give him a few shillings for a gallon of petrol. If your guest is travelling by train, then don't forget to take care also of his taxi fares and meals.

If you are inviting a speaker who devotes all his time to itinerant preaching, then obviously you have a real responsibility towards him.

> If the Gentiles have been made partakers of their spiritual things, their duty is also to minister unto them in carnal things. – Romans 15: 27.

How much should you give him? Well, why not find out what it would cost you to employ a plumber (not counting materials) at your church or home for one day, and if you think your visitor is worth more than the plumber – give him more! Don't embarrass him by handing him cash, put it in an envelope while he is there, or send him a cheque immediately after he has left, together with a brief note of appreciation.

We now come to the last of the five common characteristics of Bible Cells: Good Works, the first four being Bible Study, Prayer, Fellowship and Evangelism.

V. GOOD WORKS

Like the New Testament Church, Bible Cells today are deeply involved in practical works of kindness and mercy. When Peter addressed that evangelistic meeting in the house of Cornelius – the first Bible Cell ever planned for non-Jews – he reminded his hearers that "Jesus of Nazareth went about doing good . . . for God was with him" (Acts 10: 38).

When Zacchaeus found salvation and forgiveness through faith, he not only opened his home as a base for evangelism, and gave his witness, but immediately started making restitution, and giving to those in need!

> And Zacchaeus stood, and said unto the Lord; Behold, Lord, the half of my goods I give to the poor; and if I have taken any thing from any man by false accusation, I restore him fourfold. – Luke 19: 8.

When men really get right with God and start loving Him as they ought, they immediately start loving their fellow men – Christians and non-Christians. Moreover, this love is not mere sentiment, but is intensely practical.

> Bear ye one another's burdens, and so fulfil the law of Christ. – Galatians 6: 2.

Bear ye one another's burdens

We think of the Apostle Paul as a great preacher and theologian, and so he was; but we must not forget that he was also a great social worker and philanthropist. When he heard of the poverty, unemployment, and hunger of the saints in Jerusalem, he did *not* send them a comforting Epistle – no, he organised a relief fund, writing moving financial appeals to Christian churches to provide food for the hungry and shelter for the destitute.

It was because, in the dark ages, when men came to know God, they became concerned at the ignorance around them, and founded our great universities from whence our modern educational system springs. Others, who because they themselves were followers of the great Physician, founded our ancient hospitals. When that young society butterfly, Elizabeth Fry, turned to Christ, she devoted her life to the welfare of the wretched prisoners, and through her labour of love, the prisons of England and Europe were transformed. Through the prayers and teaching of his old nurse, Miss Millis, the young Earl of Shaftesbury became a Christian, and his love for God led him to care for the poor of London. It was because he was a Christian that William Wilber-

force, against almost overwhelming opposition, fought so courage-
ously against the slave trade. It was because he was committed
to Christ that young Dr. Barnardo cared for the homeless orphans
and started his orphanages. And what more can I say? For time
would fail me to tell of Livingstone and Carey, William Booth, and
Wilson Carlile, Moody and Whitefield, who, through faith,
emancipated slaves, fed the hungry, clothed the naked, lifted the
fallen, cared for the orphan, championed the oppressed, and healed
the sick.

Now, I am not suggesting that we should devote all our time to
'social work', neglecting prayer and the ministry of the Word,
but if we are going to be true Bible Christians, and effective
witnesses for our Lord, we must beware of becoming so heavenly
minded that we are of no earthly use.

ZEALOUS OF GOOD WORKS

One of the most significant things about many of the Bible Cells
which I have visited is their very real emphasis on this New
Testament practice of engaging in a programme of good works –
and this to my mind is yet another sign that Bible Cells are of God.

In some Cells the 'good works' are carried on quietly and
unofficially by individual members, whilst in others the entire
group plans and participates together. The variety of tasks undertaken by the Cells are legion. Let me name a few.

Forming friendships amongst the elderly and shut-ins by regular
visitation; arranging church motor transport; making and playing
recordings of sermons; undertaking chores such as cleaning,
collecting shopping; visiting hospitals, prisons, remand homes and
other institutions; helping at youth clubs, coffee bars, etc.; baby
sitting to enable young couples to attend church together; giving
to those who are in need.

SPEND TO SAVE

It is disturbing to find that many Christian people – individuals
and groups – have a very negative idea as to what the Christian
life is. For instance, many think of 'good works' only in terms of
not doing wrong, whereas the New Testament makes it clear that
good works are positive and constructive actions for the good of
others, involving self-denial of time, energy, money, home and
comfort. No man should claim to be an evangelical Christian
unless he is deeply involved with needy people – unless, under
God's guidance he is committed to a disciplined programme of

good works. These good works bring joy to our Lord, blessing to those to whom we minister, and not least, spiritual enrichment to ourselves and our group. Beyond doubt many Christians would find new spiritual life (and even physical energy) flowing into them if they started to live for others! Countless churches, yes and Bible Cells too, are bogged down spiritually because they have lost the vision of practical love and kindness!

Now, let me urge my fellow Christians to consider carefully what I am saying here. I speak to both individuals and Cells. We have the message the world needs to hear. We alone hold the divine prescription: God's remedy for sin. But there is a great gulf fixed between ourselves and the non-Christian world about us. We have lost the means of communicating the Gospel. But, thank God, there is still one bridge across – a line of communication – it is the forgotten art of Christian friendship, sympathy, kindness, and practical love. We are anxious, and rightly so, to share our faith with others, but many of us do not seem to understand that non-Christian people cannot see or understand our faith, except in so far as they see it reflected in our characters and practical actions. Talking, preaching, and arguing are worse than useless. After all, isn't this what James' letter is all about?

> Don't, I beg you, only hear the message but put it into practice. . . . If anyone appears to be 'religious' but cannot control his tongue, he deceives himself and we may be sure that his religion is useless. Religion that is pure and genuine in the sight of God the Father will show itself by such things as visiting orphans and widows in their distress and keeping oneself uncontaminated by the world. . . . Now what use is it, my brothers, for a man to say he 'has faith', if his actions do not correspond with it? Could that sort of faith save anyone's soul? If a fellow man or woman has no clothes to wear and nothing to eat, and one of you say, 'Good luck to you, I hope you'll keep warm and find enough to eat', and yet give them nothing to meet their physical needs, what on earth is the good of that? Yet that is exactly what a bare faith without a corresponding life is like – useless and dead. If we only 'have faith' a man could easily challenge us by saying, 'You say that you have faith and I have merely good actions. Well, all you can do is to show me a faith without corresponding actions, but I can show you by my actions that I have faith as well'. . . . Yes, faith without action is as dead as a body without a soul. – James 1: 22, 26, 27; 2: 14–18 and 26.

Be ye warmed and filled

Alas, there are many well-meaning Christian people who spend much of their time at crusades, conventions, Bible Studies and prayer meetings, who think only of evangelism in terms of big meetings, who never raise a finger to help the needy folk next door, but will suddenly start plastering posters everywhere and booking coaches for the Royal Albert Hall or Earls Court, and wonder why so few people show any interest, and fewer still turn to the Lord. Don't misunderstand me, no one believes more in mass evangelism than I, but mass evangelism when divorced from disciplined prayer and Christian kindness towards individuals is both unbiblical and abortive.

THE LONG-TERM POLICY

When a man takes up farming, he uses the plough and the

harrow before the harvester! Souls are not easily won to Christ. Men may produce cars by mass production methods, but souls are only conceived and quickened one by one. We must learn patience. If we would see our relatives, friends, neighbours and workmates turn to Christ, we must settle for a long-term strategic policy. We must get deeply involved not only with God and other Christians in prayer, but also with the lost in terms of Christian friendship, sympathy, kindness, and practical love.

This kind of evangelism is neither spectacular nor popular; it is, however, both scriptural and effective!

An evangelical vicar in a London suburb became deeply concerned about communicating the Gospel to the thousands of godless families in his parish. He had tried coach parties to central London rallies with little success, mainly due to the fact that his own people were not personally involved with their neighbours either in prayer or human contact, so after waiting upon God, he decided to teach his people a new kind of evangelism.

He started by calling a special meeting in his home for all those who shared his concern for their neighbours, and there he explained his spiritual strategy and long-term policy. There then followed a series of training classes held each Tuesday night, when he taught the committed Christian people how to pray for individual people and families, co-opting the covenanted prayers of others. Next he taught his people how to win the friendship and confidence of those for whom they were praying. "Try using the children," he suggested, "or the garden, the car, or holidays – use any legitimate means to get to know them, and ask them in for coffee or a meal – find out what they are interested in, and get involved with them, but remember – no preaching – just *show* them by being really good neighbours."

Towards the end of the training classes, which lasted some weeks, the vicar told his Cell:

"Now we are going to make our plans for the next phase of this operation – and this is not something *I* am going to do, but something *we* are going to do together. We are going to start planning a series of quarterly Sunday Evening Guest Services, and together we will choose the hymns and a special subject for the address. We will have invitation cards printed. There will be no public advertisements, but after much care and thought I want each of you to invite the individuals or families for whom you have been praying and working to come with you, as your guests, to the service. Naturally you will either ask them to tea before the service, or to supper afterwards. The first of these services will be held on the last Sunday of next month, so this gives us six clear weeks for praying and planning, and I don't want any of you to come that night as passengers – remember, you are working members of the crew!"

This long-term policy paid off a hundred times over; but so that you may see exactly how it worked out, let me tell you about one member of this church, and how she worked with her 'contacts' – Mr. Reader, meet Mrs. Jenkins!

HARRIET JENKINS

She is a woman in her late sixties whose husband died and left her alone in the world many years ago. She is very shy and somewhat nervous, and lives in the upstairs flat of a semi-detached house only two streets away from the church. The most important thing about Mrs. Jenkins is her saintliness. To know her is to love her. She is a woman of prayer with a deep love for the Bible but, like many another, it had never really occurred to her to try to win someone else for the Lord.

Mrs. Jenkins attended the training classes from the very start, and for the first three or four weeks she really had little idea what the vicar was getting at, and then one Tuesday 'the penny dropped!' She suddenly understood that she – Mrs. Jenkins – had a real and personal responsibility to introduce her neighbours to the Saviour Whom she loved so deeply! And as this truth gripped her, she found herself deeply shaken, and not a little frightened!

But what could *she* do? Who did *she* know? Apart from the milkman and one or two folk at the sewing party, she never met anybody! How could *she*, a nervous, shy person influence anyone for Christ? These and many more questions seemed to overwhelm her, but that night she cast her burden on the Lord. "O Lord, I know so few people, and have so few gifts, yet I do want to see others coming to know You. Who shall I pray for? Whose friendship shall I seek to win? Guide me, O Lord."

In prayer she found relief and soon afterwards was fast asleep.

Early the next morning Mrs. Jenkins went to the kitchen to make herself a cup of tea, and returning to her bedroom she put the tray down and drew back the curtains, and as she did so, she noticed that on the fence of the house opposite there was a notice, which must have been erected the previous evening: To be Sold. "Oh," she said to herself, "so they're leaving. I wonder who will come in their place?" And then, just as she stood there at the window, it hit her – it was as clear as if God spoke – indeed even clearer – the answer to her prayer – "Your new neighbours!" She went over to a drawer, took up a pen and sheet of paper, and wrote 'My new neighbours', and putting the paper in her Bible to remind herself to pray, she got back into bed, and had the best cup of tea for many a long day!

Later that week, following her minister's advice, she told her friend, Mrs. Thompson, of her experience, and together these two saintly women covenanted to pray daily, but Mrs. Jenkins not only prayed, she made her plans and watched.

About two weeks later – it was about ten o'clock one morning – Mrs. Jenkins happened to glance out of the window, and there she saw what she had been waiting for – a huge van of furniture draw up, and behind it in the family car – her new neighbours – Father, Mother, with son and daughter, both in their teens. She had seen enough! She turned round, knelt down and said a short prayer, then getting up, she put on her hat and coat, opened her desk, and took out a shopping list she had made some days before, put it in her handbag, and went off to the shops.

At half past twelve that morning, Mrs. Jenkins without ringing the bell, walked in through the open door of the house opposite, carrying a large and very heavy tray. This she took into the front room and put it down carefully on an empty packing case. It was her best tray, the solid silver coffee pot and spoons and the delicate china were all sparkling! The tray also carried the most tempting picnic lunch that you could imagine, including tasty sandwiches made of fresh white and brown bread, and oven-hot home-made scones and cakes. Every detail was perfect – and please note, for this is important, she did *not* leave a tract under the coffee pot! Just as she turned to leave, her plans seemed to break down, for her new neighbour walked into the room: "Good morning," said Mrs. Fordham, a little sharply (who isn't bad tempered when moving house!) "Can I help you?"

Covered with embarrassment, Mrs. Jenkins replied: "I am so sorry, do please forgive my walking in without being invited, but I have brought you a picnic lunch with my good wishes. I live in the flat opposite, and I know from experience how tiring a move can be. I just want you and your family to know how welcome you are here in Hillside Road. I'll come and collect the tray later – please don't bother to wash up. And if I can be of any help in any way, do please come and ask me. My name is Jenkins – Harriet Jenkins." And with this she left the house, leaving Mrs. Fordham quite speechless with her love and generosity.

Later when Mrs. Jenkins went back for the tray she was introduced to the family who peppered her with questions about the district and local tradesmen. Nothing was too much trouble, yet never for one moment did she push in where she was not wanted. She continued in earnest daily prayer, and never lost an opportunity of showing her new neighbours practical Christian love and kindness.

THE POWER OF KINDNESS

One Saturday evening about eight o'clock, about a month after the Fordhams had moved in to their new home, the door bell rang, and answering the door, Mrs. Fordham found a very agitated Mrs. Jenkins on the door step.

"I wonder if you can help me?" said the old lady – and let me assure you, Mrs. Jenkins really was agitated, she couldn't act for all the money in the world!

"Well," said Mrs. Fordham, "we'll certainly do our best. Please come in and sit down."

As the two women entered the room, Mr. Fordham and the two young people got up and welcomed their neighbour who was soon seated in a comfortable chair in the family circle. It was obvious that their friend was really worried about something.

"Now please tell us all about your problem," said Mrs. Fordham, "and we'll do our very best to help you, won't we?"

"We certainly will," said the family.

"Well, you see," said Mrs. Jenkins, "it's like this. For many years I have been a member of St. Andrew's Church – that's the old church just at the top of the road here, and I go to the services there every Sunday, except when I'm ill, of course. Well, our present vicar and his wife are both quite young, he's very nice, but he has some very modern ideas, and one of the new things which he is introducing is what he calls 'Guest Services'. I've never heard of such things before, but the idea is this. Once every quarter we plan a special service to which each member has to invite a guest, preferably someone who doesn't usually go to church, and you see I am in a great difficulty because the first of these services is tomorrow night, and I simply dare not go without taking someone else with me, and I was wondering if you would all help me by being my guests? I should like you to come over and have a cup of tea with me first. The service starts at 6.30. You will help me, won't you?"

"Why, of course we'll come," said Mrs. Fordham, "We are not very religious people ourselves, but it will do us all good to go to church for once."

Softened up by weeks of earnest, covenanted prayer, and warm-hearted Christian love and kindness, what else could the Fordhams say?

Today Mr. and Mrs. Fordham and their two young people are not only regular church-goers, but better still, fully committed Christians. It was in a home Bible Cell that they learned how to pray, study the Bible, and win others for Christ.

OBSERVE TO DO

The surest way to destroy the life and growth of a Bible Cell is for its members to be merely hearers and not doers of the Word. The study of the Scripture should never be an end in itself. We study not merely to *know*, but to *do*.

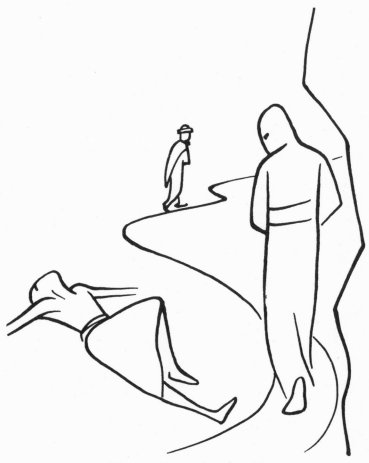

He passed by on the other side

Therefore whosoever heareth these sayings of mine, *and doeth them,* I will liken him unto a wise man, which built his house upon a rock. – Matthew 7: 24.

Yes, one of the most exciting and truly Scriptural aspects of the Bible Cells is that both individuals and groups are getting really involved in practical Christian kindness and good works, but how can anyone read the Bible without becoming involved in the needs of others, and in a disciplined life of good works?

And, behold a certain lawyer . . . willing to justify himself, said unto Jesus, And who is my neighbour? And Jesus answering said, A certain man went down from Jerusalem to Jericho, and fell among thieves, which stripped him of his raiment, and wounded him, and departed, leaving him half dead. And by chance there came down a certain priest that way: and when he saw him, he passed by on the other side. And likewise a Levite, when he was at the place, came and looked on him, and passed by on the other side. But a certain Samaritan, as he journeyed, came where he was: and when he saw him, he had compassion on him, and went to him, and bound up his wounds, pouring in oil and wine, and set him on his own beast, and brought him to an inn, and took care of him. And on the morrow when he departed, he took out two pence, and gave them to the host, and said unto him, Take care of him; and whatsoever thou spendest more, when I come again, I will repay thee. Which now of these three, thinkest thou, was neighbour unto him that fell among the thieves? And he said, He that shewed mercy on him. Then said Jesus unto him, Go, and do thou likewise. – Luke 10: 25–37.

It is so much easier to give a man a tract than to get personally involved in his interests and problems, but nowhere near so effective. It requires far less effort to organise a coach party to attend a giant evangelistic rally than to pray persistently for the conversion of six personal friends or relations. It costs far less to send a big cheque to an evangelist or a society than to open your heart and home to your non-Christian neighbours.

Before you win a man's soul, you must first win his confidence. This was the Master's technique. The Gospels are full of examples of this.

These then are the five common characteristics of Bible Cells which I have seen throughout the world: Bible Study, Prayer, Fellowship, Evangelism, and Good Works.

How to start a Bible Cell

IF you are not already involved in the fellowship of a living Cell, I pray that by now you will be asking the question: "How can I start a Bible Cell?" This important question is easy to ask, but difficult to answer. One of the many enquiries I have made in my various journeys has been: "How exactly did your Bible Cell start?" The answers I have received have been legion, and it may help if I quote some of them.

"About three years ago my wife and I were sitting one evening in our lounge talking with a Christian couple we know, and in course of conversation we discovered that they, like ourselves, were starved for Christian fellowship and the Word of God, when suddenly Martin's wife, Jane, looked up and said: 'Well, why don't we do something about it, rather than sit here and talk? Can't we read a passage of the Bible together and pray all round?' And that's what we did. We enjoyed ourselves so much that we have been meeting regularly ever since. Others have joined us, and our Bible Cell has been the means of transforming our Christian lives."

"Well, as you know our Cell consists almost exclusively of bachelor girls who meet each Thursday in Marjorie and Anne's flat. I first heard of Bible Cells when I was on holiday several years ago, and because there is no evangelical church in our area, several of us started meeting for prayer and Bible study, and although our numbers have not increased very much (our average number is nine or ten) we have all grown greatly in grace and knowledge through the fellowship of the Group."

"Our Bible Cell started first as a Women's Prayer Group in connection with one of Billy Graham's Crusades. Several of the women for whom we prayed at that time turned to the Lord, and then joined us for follow-up in simple Bible studies. Our numbers have grown steadily. We have had to divide several times. There are now six or seven lively Bible Cells in our neighbourhood, each of which God is using greatly."

"We are fortunate in belonging to a Bible-based church, and we are indebted to our minister for telling us about Bible Cells. Our church Bible study had been poorly attended for some years, so he called several couples together, including ourselves, and told us of his idea for Bible Cells. Each group studies the same passage every week, and whereas only about 20 or 25 would attend a formal midweek Bible reading at the church, we now have far more than treble that number meeting in Home Bible Cell Groups."

"Jack and I went to Hildenborough Hall for our summer holiday three or four years ago, and there we heard how God was working through Home Bible Cells. When we came home, we prayed about it together, asking for God's guidance. We then dedicated ourselves, and our home, afresh to Him. After a while we felt we should invite two other Christian couples, and we told them how we felt, and together the six of us decided that we would meet each Sunday evening at 8 o'clock for Bible study and prayer, and this we have done now during the past few years. Not only have our own lives been greatly enriched, but through earnest prayer, practical kindness, patience, and love, we have seen several of our neighbours also turning to Christ."

"My brother-in-law from Scotland came to stay with us, and we were telling him how completely starved we were for solid Bible teaching and Christian fellowship. He then told us how God had been blessing him, and a group of his friends through a Home Bible Study Group. We then peppered him with questions, and through this conversation my husband and I were inspired to call together a few like-minded people, and after prayer we started meeting regularly. It is not easy, because we lack experienced leadership, but we are all getting to know the Bible better, and what is more, two or three other couples have become Christians."

These are some of the many varied answers I have received in reply to my question: "How did your Bible Cell start?"

PRAY FIRST – PLAN AFTER

Now, if you feel that the Holy Spirit is guiding you to start a Bible Cell, either in your own home, or in a neighbour's, let me urge you first to pray privately and earnestly that in all things you may be guided by God. It is so easy for us to make plans, and then when our plans are finalised, to seek His blessing on the plans we have made. This is the wrong way round. We should first seek His direction, and then we may be confident that in His will we shall enjoy His blessing. His commands are His enablings. He does not give strength for uncommanded tasks. Peter Marshall once prayed: "Lord, save us from hot heads and cold feet, Amen." We must never rush ahead of God in the energy of the flesh, nor lag behind through unbelief.

If, as you pray privately, the pressure of the Spirit increases, then it might be wise for you to call one or two other like-minded people, and open your heart to them concerning your burden. Don't ask them to make plans, but invite them to join you in praying for the guidance of the Holy Spirit. Remember, God is never in any hurry, and 'he that believeth shall not make haste' – Isaiah 28: 16. Having discussed the matter and given them fuel for prayer, pray together, then decide to meet again and if it seems good to you and the Holy Spirit to proceed, there are a number of matters that you would have to consider:

(a) Who should be invited to join the Cell?
(b) Where and when should you meet?
(c) How regularly should the Cell meet?
(d) How long should each meeting last?
(e) Who should be the leader of the Group? Should one leader be appointed for say six weeks, or should you take it in turns to lead?
(f) Should you have any refreshments?
(g) And last, but by no means least, how many sessions should you arrange?

Make your plans for a limited period only. You are not forming a new denomination (God forbid!), you are merely planning a series of experimental, informal home meetings. There are innumerable Christian meetings, societies, yes, and churches which have long since outlived their usefulness. When a Bible Cell ceases to be truly effective in strengthening Christians and making Christ known, if it cannot be revived, then it should be allowed to die, and be given a respectable burial!

Let me urge you to avoid any kind of publicity. The technique of Bible Cell evangelism is very different from that of mass evangelism. In mass evangelism the more publicity, the better; in Bible Cell evangelism, the less publicity, the better. Bible Cells should grow steadily, quietly, and unobtrusively like a living seed.

Move one step at a time. Ask God to make you and your friends sensitive to the guidance of His Spirit. God seldom guides two Bible Cells either to start or develop along the same lines.

LIVING CELLS DIVIDE

The communist cells which are so effective in spreading the doctrines of Karl Marx are never allowed to become too big. They have proved that several small cells are far more effective than one large one. Therefore, when the membership rises to a certain level, the cell automatically divides. This technique was not invented by Karl Marx, or his fellow travellers, but was the method laid down in the New Testament by our Lord for the propagation of His gospel. In these days of mass communications, alas, many Christian people gauge the effectiveness of a church, crusade, or Bible Cell only in terms of numbers. This is reflected in the first question that most people ask about any Christian gathering: "How many were there?" There are many things far more important than numbers – a sense of God's Presence, the clarity of the Word, and an attentive congregation.

Like many a modern Christian warrior, Gideon had to learn that numbers signify very little in the economy of God. The whole technique of Bible Cell evangelism is completely contrary to the method in which the majority of evangelical Christians have been trained.

As soon as your Cell numbers more than twelve, you should consider prayerfully the advisability of some members hiving off and forming another Cell. This suggestion will be resisted both by those who are mainly concerned with numbers, and those who have little confidence in the guidance and teaching of the Holy Spirit.

When the Cell has divided, or subdivided, the members of the various Cells throughout the area should keep in touch with one another, meeting together once a month, or once a quarter for thanksgiving, fellowship, and prayer. On these occasions a special speaker is often invited to expound a passage of Scripture or give a stirring word of exhortation.

ASKING THE MINISTER

Christian people prayerfully considering starting a Bible Cell often ask: "What about our Minister? Do we go and discuss it with him, or just go ahead?" The answer to this question depends almost entirely upon your minister. In view of the plain teaching of the Bible, it is remarkable to find many Christian people who imagine that because a man calls himself 'Rev.', 'Pastor', 'Father', or 'Evangelist', he is therefore necessarily a man of God. The solemn warnings given by our Lord should be carefully observed.

> Beware of false prophets (preachers), which come to you in sheep's clothing, but inwardly they are ravening wolves. . . .
> Many will say to me in that day, Lord, Lord, have we not prophesied (preached) in Thy Name? and in Thy Name have cast out devils? and in Thy Name done many wonderful works? And then will I profess unto them, I never knew

you: depart from me, ye that work iniquity. – Matthew
7: 15, 22, 23.
But he answered and said, Every plant, which my heavenly
Father hath not planted, shall be rooted up. Let them
alone: they be blind leaders of the blind. And if the blind
lead the blind, both shall fall into the ditch. – Matthew
15: 13, 14.

The Apostle John gives a similar warning:

Beloved, believe not every spirit, but try the spirits
whether they are of God: because many false prophets
(preachers) are gone out into the world. – 1 John 4: 1.

Before entrusting the health of your body to a doctor, you first
satisfy yourself that he is a qualified physician. Before entrusting
the education of your mind to a teacher, you make sure that he
is fully qualified. It is sheer folly to entrust the care of your soul
to a minister who is but a wolf in sheep's clothing, or a blind leader
of the blind, a false prophet.

In deciding whether or not you should discuss the proposed
Bible Cell with your minister, ask yourself these questions: "Does
he show every evidence of being a really converted man?" "Does
he constantly affirm the Deity, the Atonement and Resurrection
of our Lord Jesus Christ?" "Does he genuinely believe in, and
faithfully expound the Word of God?" "Does he preach for
conversions?" "Are men and women truly converted to Christ,
and do they follow on to know the Lord through his ministry?"
If the answer to these important questions is an emphatic 'yes',
then I think you have a duty to your minister to share with him
the plans you have in mind, and seek his prayerful support. If I
were a minister, and heard that members of my congregation
were meeting in their own homes to read the Word of God and
pray, I would fall on my knees and thank God fervently. And if
your minister does not do the same, then there must be something
seriously wrong with him – or you!

This question as to whether you should discuss your Bible Cell
with your minister depends very largely on whether your Cell is
to be organised privately, or as a church activity. If the latter,
then obviously you must first discuss the matter fully with your
minister, and the church officers concerned, and not proceed
without obtaining their approval. If, on the other hand, your Cell
is to be organised privately by invitation only, then it is primarily
the responsibility of your family, not of your minister. After all,
members of a church do not normally ask their minister if they

can give a private dinner party, coffee morning, or social evening, and all you are planning to do is to invite in a few personal friends to your home to talk about the things of God.

THE CHURCH-BASED BIBLE CELL

Scores of ministers, true men of God, drawn from every conceivable Protestant denomination all over the world, bear testimony to the tremendous blessing Bible Cells have been not only to their congregation, but to non-church-going families in the neighbourhood.

The experience of my friend, the Rev. Lorimer Caldwell, is typical of many. Mr. Caldwell is a spiritually minded man with a deep love for the Lord Jesus. He is an outstanding pastor and expositor. There is no other church within twenty miles where the Word of God is faithfully preached. Mr. Caldwell was called to his church some six years ago, and he continued the tradition of a Wednesday Evening Midweek Bible Reading, and although his Sunday congregations averaged between 500 and 600 people, the Wednesday Evening Bible Exposition was attended by only thirty faithful people. This poor attendance naturally concerned my friend, and in spite of his earnest prayers, showed no sign of increase. Then, after prayerful consideration he called a number of his praying people together, and told them of his plan. With the utmost care he selected twelve Christian couples, varying in age from newly marrieds to the retired folk. These people were drawn from various parts of the town. They were all spiritually minded people, and many of them well taught in the Word, and there in the manse he shared with them the vision that God had given him for Bible Cells throughout the town, and he asked these couples if they would be willing to open their homes at 8 o'clock for the next ten Wednesday evenings for Home Bible Study Groups. Moreover, he asked them if they would be willing to meet him at the manse each Friday evening so that he might pray with them, and go through with them the passage that was to be discussed the following Wednesday. Some of these people were a little hesitant, but only two or three failed to comply with his request. After some preliminary training for the leaders, Mr. Caldwell gave the addresses of the homes where Bible Cells were being held, and invited people to attend the Cell nearest to their home. Some of the Cells were crowded out, they had more people than they wanted. A few of them where disappointingly small, but after three or four weeks the numbers settled down, and everyone was tremendously enthusiastic about the results. Many learned to pray aloud in public for the first time; others became deeply interested in the Bible, and learnt how to study it for themselves in their own homes. A new spirit of fellowship sprang up in the Church, and best of all, many non-Christians found new life in Christ.

The Bible Cells in this church have now been running for just over three years, and Mr. Caldwell tells me that there are ten flourishing Cells, each with an average attendance of fifteen people, "and whereas thirty people came reluctantly to my Midweek Service, we now have 150 people studying the Bible in small groups for themselves." Needless to say the minister keeps in close touch with the leaders, and is always ready to call on any new contacts that are made through the Cells. From time to time he spends an evening with the leaders for prayer and consultation. During the first ten weeks experimental period he and his wife led their own group in the manse, but recently he has found it more useful to drop in on a different Cell each Wednesday evening.

No, this does not mean that he has given up his expository preaching. Both Sunday morning and evening he continues this invaluable work, but he tells me that quite a number of new people have joined his church, and his Sunday congregations have grown considerably as a result of the Bible Cells in his parish.

SUNDAY EVENING SERVICE

Another friend of mine, who is also a faithful minister of the gospel, draws large congregations on Sunday morning, but finds that on Sunday evening the numbers are growing smaller and smaller. He is therefore, with his church leaders, discussing the possibility of closing the Sunday evening service, and instead opening Bible Cells in the homes of the people. He thinks that the young people will get together in one home and do little more than have a hearty sing-song, the university students are anxious to debate knotty theological problems, while others feel that the emphasis should be laid on prayer and Bible study.

I have talked to innumerable ministerial groups throughout Britain and America about the Bible Cell movement, and occasionally I have come across ministers who see a grave danger of splinter groups arising from home-based Bible Cells. There are, no doubt, certain dangers in this method of evangelism which should be carefully watched, but this is true in every form of outreach, particularly where lay people are encouraged to use their initiative and assume responsibility. The true minister not only does the work of an evangelist and teacher, but also trains his people that they in turn may train and teach others. This was the Master's method; this was the Apostles' method:

> And the things that thou hast heard of me among many witnesses, the same commit thou to faithful men, who shall be able to teach others also. – 2 Timothy 2: 2.

D. L. Moody used to say that the man who sets ten men to work is far more use to God than the man who does ten men's work.

Every minister who has worked enthusiastically with Bible Cells in his congregation speaks in glowing terms of their effectiveness.

A number of ministers have invited a small team of people, who have had experience of Bible Cells, to come to their churches and tell their people of what God is doing. This gives the minister and his people an opportunity of asking questions, and finding out whether or not Bible Cells could be used in their own congregation.

Every minister would be well advised to experiment with Bible Cells in his church for a set period of time, say for three or six months, making it clear to his people at the outset that it is not necessarily a permanent feature.

Some folk do not realise that there are many towns, indeed whole districts, where there is virtually no evangelical Bible witness. Because God does not leave Himself without a witness nor suffer His people to go unfed, He is, I believe, bringing into being, throughout the world, countless home-based Bible Cells, and using them to the upbuilding of His people, and the extension of His Kingdom.

The Leader

THE leader of a Bible Cell is an important person, whether he be the permanent leader, or chairman for one evening. A poor leader can easily cause the death of a Cell. On the other hand, the right man can be used of God, not only to the spiritual development of those in his Cell, but to the conversion of many non-Christians, and the formation of numerous new Cells. Perhaps I can best describe a good leader by first describing what he is *not*.

● A good Bible Cell leader is *not* a dictator. He is not there to bully and regiment his fellow members. He is not a driver, but a leader. The Cell does not exist for him, but he exists for the Cell. Indeed, for Christ's sake he is the servant of all (Matthew 23: 8-12; 2 Corinthians 4: 5).

● A good Bible Cell leader is *not* a preacher, lecturer, or teacher. Whilst collecting material for this book, a Christian minister kindly invited me to 'sit in' on a home discussion group he had planned in connection with his church. The group met in a home on a large housing estate. Our hostess welcomed us with a warm smile, a cup of tea, and a biscuit, then the minister asked us to be

Apt to teach

seated. He then introduced me, and asked me to open the study with prayer. Immediately afterwards he rose to his feet, and opened a large Bible, and said: "This week we are continuing our studies in the book of Leviticus," and then for more than three-quarters of an hour he gave us a heavy Bible exposition, and then closed with the benediction. There was no opportunity given for anyone else to take part, even in asking questions. I had a similar experience in the United States.

Both of these meetings were wrongly described as 'Home Bible Study Groups'. The exposition of Scripture is very important, but the purpose of a Home Study Group is that the members may participate. The leader's job is not to teach or to talk, but rather to get others to do the studying and speaking. He should be as self-effacing as possible, yet bear in mind that the Holy Spirit works through dedicated human leadership and personality.

● A good Bible Cell leader is *not* a saint with a bee in his bonnet! Alas, many ministers and laymen use their position of leadership to further their own favourite doctrines or religious experiences. If the devil cannot make us backsliders, he will endeavour to make us cranks who can no longer see the wood for the trees. A good leader will make it his duty to see that his Cell is kept on the main line of balanced, Biblical truth, and is never diverted into a siding of any particular aspect of truth or Christian experience, no matter how important he feels them to be. Any truth emphasised to the exclusion of other truths becomes a heresy.

● A good Bible Cell leader is *never* rude. If someone in the group gets hold of the wrong end of the stick, he will never rebuke him before others. In a hesitating way, he will say "Yes [it is possible to say 'yes' in such a way that it means 'no'] – has someone else another idea on this?" The good leader is always appreciative. "Yes, that's an excellent thought, that has never occurred to me before."

● A good Bible Cell leader is *not* necessarily a trained theologian, or an experienced Bible student. Indeed, it is sometimes better if the leader himself is learning along with the group, for he is more likely to encourage others to participate. The group that is constantly led by a theologian tends to become an appreciative audience, rather than a living Cell.

THE LEADER'S RESPONSIBILITY

● It is the responsibility of the leader to pray daily and earnestly

144

that the session for which he is responsible may be guided and blessed by God the Holy Spirit.

● To read the passage of Scripture, which is to be studied, prayerfully and carefully, not only in the Authorised Version, but also in other versions, to search for parallel Scriptures, which might be overlooked by others during the study; to look out any interesting or relevant background to the passage, to ascertain the correct pronunciation of difficult words, to prepare carefully a brief introduction to the passage (model introductions are given on pages 21 and 48). He should never hesitate to seek the help of good Commentaries, or the advice of a more experienced Bible student. His introduction should either be written out fully, or his notes carefully prepared. He must decide well in advance what he is going to do about prayer: Will he get one person to lead in prayer? If so, he must ask them to do so in good time. Is he going to throw the meeting open to anyone to pray? Pass the Bible round? These details must be settled during his preparation time. He must decide how the Scripture is to be read. If he decides to ask one person to read the Scripture, he should give ample time to prepare the reading. Or, will they read alternate verses with himself, or read round? He must find out what announcements are to be made about forthcoming meetings.

● To arrive at the home where the meeting is to be held at least fifteen minutes before starting time, to make sure that those who are responsible for refreshments, chairs, Bibles, notebooks, pencils, etc., have not failed in their assignments.

● To make sure, if refreshments are being served before the study commences, that the tea, coffee, and biscuits are served to guests immediately they arrive. He should not, of course, attempt to undertake these tasks himself, but delegate the work to others.

● To make each member of the group feel thoroughly at home, making sure that the newcomers are properly introduced and made really welcome.

● To make sure that each member of the group has a Bible for his exclusive use. Two people sharing the same Bible will spoil the session for both.

● To resist the temptation to 'give the late-comers another few minutes'. Even if only half the Group have arrived, or his hostess has a mouthful of biscuit, precisely on the appointed hour he should take his place, and with a happy, yet firm voice, say: "It is

8 o'clock – please will everyone be seated. It is my duty to see that the meeting starts and ends promptly."

● To be completely relaxed, knowing that he has done his utmost in prayer and preparation, and is relying upon the Holy Spirit to guide the group in their meditation, discussion, and prayer. A relaxed and happy leader makes for a relaxed and happy group.

● To speak in a natural tone of voice. A surprising number of Christian people seem to pull out the 'holy tremolo' stop when they speak of spiritual things.

● To avoid at all costs the language of Zion, and Christian clichés, and speak in terms that ordinary people can understand. He should not talk of people as 'the dear unsaved', but as 'non-Christians', not 'Charles has come through', but 'Charles has turned to Christ', not 'this morning during my quiet time', but 'this morning when I was praying'.

● To give a brief exhortation to the Cell, after prayer and the reading of Scripture, such as "Once again we turn to the Holy Scriptures. We are not coming to criticise the Bible, but to be criticised by it. We are not here to teach each other, but rather to learn of God. We are not here to forward our own thoughts and ideas, but to be taught of God through the Bible, and one another. We will not waste time discussing whether the Bible is true or not. We will accept it as we have it in front of us. Let each of us purpose in our heart to do all we can to help others. Now, by way of introduction to tonight's passage . . ." His introduction should be as brief, and as concise as possible, four minutes at the outside. He should resist the temptation to include anything which is likely to be brought out by others in the course of the discussion. At the earliest possible moment he should 'pass the ball' to the other members of the Group for meditation and participation. As the captain is always the last to leave his ship, so the leader should keep back his own thoughts until the others have had an opportunity of taking part.

● To make certain that the Group keeps strictly to the point, and for this task he will need the wisdom of Solomon, the patience of Job, the courage of Daniel, and the strength of Samson. No matter how interesting other topics may be, no matter how unpopular he may make himself, whenever a member of the Group deviates from the Scripture under consideration, the leader must call the meeting back to order immediately with a firm hand.

● To turn questions to the group. When anyone asks a question, even if the leader knows the answer, he should first pass the question over to the group: "Who can help John with this problem?" This encourages others to think and participate. After others have spoken, the leader might say: "I think the answer to John's question lies in the fact that. . . ." Whatever happens, the leader should never lose any opportunity of confessing his ignorance. To say: "I really don't know the answer to that one" may be difficult, but it is often very true and always helpful.

● To encourage the timid to take part, taking care never to cause any embarrassment. This he can do in several ways. For instance, after the silent meditation, he may say: "Now, has anyone any special thought they would like to share with us on this verse?" Even as he speaks, he will look in the direction of someone who has not yet taken part, and very slightly raise his eyebrows – sometimes the eyes speak more eloquently than the lips. Or again, if a simple or obvious answer is before the group, he could turn to 'Timid Tim' and say: "Tim, have you got any idea what the answer might be?"

● To restrain the over-talkative member of the group. A good plan to keep 'Mr. Talkative' quiet, and to encourage 'Mr. Timid' to speak up, is for the leader to say: "Now, we'll turn to the verse 7, and after our silent prayer and meditation I am going to ask only those who have not yet taken part in the discussion this evening to give us their thoughts." If this fails, the leader can always say: "Now anyone is free to join in." If 'Mr. Talkative' continues to monopolise the discussion, then for the sake of the group, at the risk of offending 'Mr. Talkative' too, the leader should speak to him privately, telling him how much his help is appreciated, but pointing out that it would help the group considerably if he would not take part so often, or if he could keep his helpful comments really brief. The question is not, will this task be pleasant or unpleasant to the leader, or to 'Mr. Talkative', but what will be best for the group.

● To see that a good balance is being kept by the Cell. Are they giving too much attention, or too little attention, to parallel verses? Are they concentrating too much on the finer points of doctrine, and neglecting the down-to-earth application of the Scriptures to their personal lives, or vice versa?

● To see that no discussion, however relevant or important, degenerates into anything approaching an argument. The object of a Bible Cell is not to win arguments, but to win men for Christ.

● To keep his eye on the clock, to make sure there is time left, before the conclusion of the session, for prayer arising out of the evening's study.

● To see that the group is given details of the next week's session, the name of the leader, the time and the place of the meeting, and, if the group think it helpful, the passage to be studied.

The servant of the Lord must not strive

PHYSICAL ARRANGEMENTS
The Meeting Place

Virtually every Cell I have visited has found that it is far better to meet in a private home rather than on church premises. Some always meet in the same home, whilst others move from house to house. Cells do not all meet in Christian homes; indeed there is much to be said for using a fringe or non-Christian home particularly for outreach meetings. The venue should be easy to find, and within easy reach of the members, and for the normal meeting, large enough to accommodate between ten and twenty people.

The Chairs

The arrangement of the chairs is of considerable importance. They should not be placed in straight rows as for a lecture, but informally round the room, so that whoever is taking part can be seen easily by the entire group. The leader's chair should be in a conspicuous place to help him command attention. Some groups sit round a large table, finding it easy for spreading their books and making notes. Empty seats should be left near the door for latecomers. Co-opt the help of one or two able-bodied men to arrive early and put the chairs in position, and be responsible for putting them back at the close of the session. The leader and the members of the group should remain seated during the discussion.

Hats and Coats

Plans should be made in advance for one or two to arrive in good time to open the door to their fellow members, showing them where to leave their hats and coats, welcoming newcomers, and introducing them to members of the Cell.

Heating and Ventilation

Care should be given both to the heating and the ventilation of the room. Each human body gives off heat equivalent to that of a small electric fire, so it is better to start with the room too cold than too hot. An adequate supply of fresh air will help to prevent people feeling drowsy.

Lighting

Check the lighting; see that it is not too fierce, so that folk are dazzled, and not too dim so that they cannot see to read their Bibles.

Bibles and Notebooks

Several extra Bibles should be available at each session for those who come without their own. Make sure that newcomers are not embarrassed. Always announce either the Bible page number, or exactly where and how to find the passage under discussion. Some Cells provide notebooks and pencils for members who like to make notes.

Refreshments

These should be thought out and organised well in advance. Co-opt others to help, and thus get them involved. The majority of groups prefer to start off with refreshments, rather than having them at the end. Make sure that your hostess is not left to tidy up and wash the cups and saucers after the group has gone.

It is of the utmost importance that the refreshments be kept as simple as possible. There should be a choice of tea or coffee. Sandwiches, cakes, or pastries should not be served. The only food available should be biscuits (cookies). One Cell which moved week by week from house to house for its normal meetings was faced with quite a problem. The hostesses vied with one another as to which could put on the most exotic refreshments! It is important that even in a small group there should be a treasurer, and even though the hostess is more than willing to provide the refreshments, pay for the milk, coffee and biscuits herself, other members of the Bible Cell should contribute to this expense, for the simple reason that in some other home, expense might be quite a consideration, and if it is the rule for the refreshments to be paid for from the funds, there will be no future embarrassment.

A table should be set up near the door, and each member should help himself to what he requires. This means that every precious moment can be taken up with intelligent conversation.

Personal Discipline

THE spiritual life and effectiveness of a Bible Cell is determined entirely by that of the individual member.

> If every member was just like me,
> What sort of Bible Cell would my Cell be?

The original followers of the Lord Jesus were known as 'disciples'. It was a considerable time before they were given the name of 'Christians'.

> And the disciples were called Christians first in Antioch. – Acts 11 : 26.

The word 'disciple' corresponds roughly with our modern words scholar, student, or learner. The original idea of the word was one who was under the discipline of another, and strictly speaking a true Christian is one who is under the discipline of his Master, not merely one who is trusting Him in a vague, general sense.

The greatest weakness in the Church today is that the individual Christian lacks personal discipline. An army is not likely to succeed on the battlefield unless the officers and men have first learnt discipline. Again and again the Master made it clear that following Him involved extreme personal sacrifice. Ponder these words:

> If any person wills to come after me, let him deny himself – that is, disown himself and his own interests, and take up his cross daily, and follow me, cleave steadfastly to me, conform wholly to my example. – Luke 9: 23 (Amplified Bible).

Our love for Christ must be so great that our love for others, even our nearest and dearest, must be hatred by comparison.

> If any man come to me, and hate not his father, and mother, and wife, and children, and brethren, and sisters, yea, and his own life also, he cannot be my disciple. – Luke 14: 26.

Yes, discipleship involves a daily saying *no* to ourselves and *yes* to Christ. We must give up all right to ourselves, and recognise every moment of every day that in thought, word and deed we are not our own, we are bought with a price (1 Corinthians 6: 19, 20).

The New Testament knows nothing of what Reginald Wallis

used to call 'Easy Believeism'. The Apostles insisted that the Jesus Whom they preached was not only Saviour, but Lord, "a Prince and a Saviour" (Acts 5: 31).

The modern notion that to be a Christian, a man need only 'believe' and then go away and live as he pleases is utterly foreign to the teaching of our Lord and His Apostles. To be a Christian, a man must deny himself not only flagrant sin, but also worldly things – things both dirty and doubtful.

The only Christian faith known in the New Testament is the belief that behaves, the creed that governs conduct.

> What good is it, my brethren, if a man professes to have faith, and yet his actions do not correspond? Can such faith save him? – James 2: 14.

But being a disciple of Jesus Christ involves not only sacrificing those things which are sinful and worldly in our lives, but more especially it involves discipline in adding those things which are lacking.

> And beside this, giving all diligence, add to your faith virtue; and to virtue knowledge; and to knowledge temperance; and to temperance patience; and to patience godliness; and to godliness brotherly kindness; and to brotherly kindness charity. For if these things be in you, and abound, they make you that ye shall neither be barren nor unfruitful in the knowledge of our Lord Jesus Christ. But he that lacketh these things is blind, and cannot see afar off, and hath forgotten that he was purged from his old sins. – 2 Peter 1: 5–9.

Paul reminds us that the whole purpose of redemption is not merely negative, but also positive. We are not only saved from iniquity, but to good works.

> The great God and our Saviour Jesus Christ; Who gave Himself for us, that He might redeem us from all iniquity, and purify unto Himself a peculiar people, zealous of good works. . . . These things I will that thou affirm constantly, that they which have believed in God might be careful to maintain good works. – Titus 2: 13, 14; 3: 8.

I cannot here enumerate the many good works which in the New Testament we are constantly exhorted to put into practice, but I want to name seven important things which are clearly set forth – things which, if they are missing, make our Christian lives barren and unfruitful. If a Bible Cell is to be effective, each true

Christian member should be committed to this Biblical seven-point Plan for Disciplined Christian Living. The order in which I set out these things has no bearing upon their importance.

I. DISCIPLINE IN PRAYER

Praying is as vital to spiritual life as breathing is to physical life. No man has a right to call himself a Christian who does not commune with God every day in prayer. Each of the four gospel writers pictures our Lord as a man of prayer, and I must not – dare not – call myself His disciple unless in this I follow His holy example.

And he withdrew himself into the wilderness, and prayed. – Luke 5: 16.

He was constantly teaching His disciples to pray, not only by giving explicit instructions, but also by permitting them to listen whilst He was at prayer.

Apart from setting us the example in prayer, He commanded us, His followers, to pray:

When thou prayest, enter into thy closet, and when thou hast shut thy door, pray to thy Father which is in secret. – Matthew 6: 6.

And he told them a parable, to the effect that they ought always to pray and not lose heart. – Luke 18: 1.

Although New Testament believers are set free from the burden of the ceremonial law once incumbent upon the Jews, we must understand clearly that we are still subject to the law of Christ.

If you love me, you will keep my commandments. . . . He who has my commandments, and keeps them, he it is who loves me. . . . If a man loves me, he will keep my word. . . . He who does not love me does not keep my words. – John 14: 15, 21, 23, 24.

One of the 'commandments', 'sayings', 'words' of the Master was that we, His disciples, should always pray. Prayerlessness therefore is not weakness – it is SIN. The Apostle James makes it clear that there are not only sins of commission – doing those things I ought not to do – but also sins of omission – leaving undone those things I ought to do.

Therefore to him that knoweth to do good, and doeth it not, to him it is sin. – James 4: 17.

One of the most solemn verses to be found anywhere in scripture concerning prayer is the word of Samuel to the men of Israel:

God forbid that I should sin against the Lord in ceasing to pray for you. – I Samuel 12: 23.

The Christian who is too busy to pray is just too busy. John Wesley said: "There has been so much to do of late that I have had to spend more time in prayer." The man who prays most, helps most. Prayer is not my getting my will done in heaven; it is getting God's will done here on earth. Prayer does not change God's plan; it merely releases His Power on earth. There is nothing so tiring, yet so refreshing, as prayer. Prayer, above everything else, brings pleasure to the heart of my Lord, blessing to my fellow men, and refreshment to my own soul. Preaching is limited in its power and influence, but there is no man or woman on earth who cannot be touched by praying.

Have you ever noticed how easy it is to plan, to organise and work, yet the moment you kneel to pray, the devil seems to thwart you; you are reminded of an urgent task, the telephone rings, or you are suddenly conscious of physical exhaustion.

What various hindrances we meet
In coming to the mercy-seat!
Yet who, that knows the worth of prayer,
But wishes to be often there!

Prayer makes the darkened cloud withdraw,
Prayer climbs the ladder Jacob saw,
Gives exercise to faith and love,
Brings every blessing from above.

Restraining prayer, we cease to fight;
Prayer makes the Christian's armour bright;
And Satan trembles when he sees
The weakest saint upon his knees.

While Moses stood with arms spread wide,
Success was found on Israel's side;
But when, through weariness, they failed,
That moment Amalek prevailed.

– William Cowper.

Prayer – Privilege and Duty

Innumerable helpful books have been written and sermons

preached on the subject of prayer, but in final analysis the only way to learn how to pray – is to pray. Many of us ought not to be praying: "Lord, teach me *how* to pray", but rather, "Lord, teach me *to* pray!"

Prayer is not only a privilege, but a solemn duty. We must pray not only when we feel like it, but when we don't feel like it! Some people talk a lot of pious nonsense about our only praying when we feel led to do so, but if most of us only prayed when we 'felt led' I fear our prayers would be few and far between! The mature Christian should never allow his prayer life to be influenced by his feelings, but should learn to influence his feelings by his prayer life. God's guidance is never contrary to our duty, and therefore to fail in our duty is to disobey His guidance.

The Psalmist disciplined himself in the matter of prayer:

Evening, and morning, and at noon, will I pray. – Psalm 55: 17.

The vast majority of Christians, like their Lord, find that the best time for prayer is in the early morning:

And in the morning, rising up a great while before day, he went out, and departed into a solitary place, and there prayed. – Mark 1: 35.

Having discussed the battle of prayer with innumerable numbers of people, I am convinced that for the majority of us, we either pray right at the beginning of the day or we do not pray at all!

More than likely you have to start work at a set time. Supposing it is 9 o'clock. You know that it takes you half an hour to get up, dress, and have breakfast, and another half an hour to get to work, and therefore if your alarm is set to go off at 8 o'clock, you just cannot pray – there is no time. But as a committed, disciplined Christian, you just cannot behave like this. You must learn to say 'no' to that that extra half-hour in bed. That alarm clock must go off not a second later than 7.30, and the moment you hear it ring, seize those blankets, fling them back, and cry: "Depart from me ye workers of iniquity," then as quickly as possible wash and dress yourself, and spend an absolute minimum of thirty minutes' unhurried communion with God. Learn to say no to yourself; no prayer – no porridge; no Bible – no breakfast. But don't imagine you will be able to discipline yourself in the early morning if you indulge yourself at night watching the late TV show!

The true disciple of Jesus Christ should give God not less than thirty minutes every day for private prayer. This discipline in prayer will transform the spiritual life of your Bible Cell, and it will enrich your own life beyond telling.

> Drop Thy still dews of quietness,
> Till all our strivings cease:
> Take from our souls the strain and stress:
> And let our ordered lives confess
> The beauty of Thy peace.

I have met Christian people from time to time who speak disparagingly of what they call 'the fetish of the Quiet Time', but in my life and broad experience of talking to Christian people, I am convinced that the majority of folk are spiritually barren and ineffective because they do not meet with God in a regular, disciplined manner. The exhortation of Paul "Let all things be done decently and in order" should be applied not only to public worship, but also to our private devotions.

The Prayer List

There are some people whose social circle is particularly small, or whose memory is phenomenally large, who can intercede effectively for their Christian friends and unbelieving neighbours without the aid of a prayer list, but the vast majority of intelligent scholars in the school of prayer find a prayer list indispensable. No doubt a prayer list presents serious problems, but the lack of one presents far more.

Invest in an attractive, good quality loose-leaf pocket book, and set aside a page or so for people, problems, and situations about which you feel you should pray daily, then take seven other pages, one for each day of the week, and divide amongst these pages the names of people for whom you should pray. No doubt you will want to remember your immediate relatives and close friends, and that short list of folk for whose conversion you are praying daily, then perhaps you will scatter throughout the days of the week the names of those who are sick, bereaved, elderly, lonely, and distressed. You will no doubt want to remember too your minister, missionary friends, Christian doctors and nurses, your own church with its various organisations, the various countries of the world, Christian youth organisations, Christian orphanages, social workers, medical and city missions, evangelists, Bible teachers those who work amongst students, children, and social drop-outs.

I have one or two old Bibles and hymn books, and when I come across a helpful Psalm, passage of Scripture, or hymn, I cut these out and paste them in my loose-leaf book. These I find to be of inestimable value. Bear in mind that the strength of your Bible Cell or church depends entirely upon the effectiveness of your private prayers.

II. DISCIPLINE IN BIBLE STUDY

To the man who would make a success of the Christian life, a prayerful, disciplined, systematic study of the Bible is absolutely essential. No man has ever become a successful physicist, surgeon, geologist, or astronomer who did not study his textbooks diligently, nor can any man hope to make a success of the Christian life who neglects his textbook – the Holy Bible.

I have been a Christian for many years, during which time I have travelled extensively, and met many thousands of Christian people in all walks of life, and I learned long ago that a man's attitude towards Jesus Christ can be gauged by his attitude to the Bible. The man who reverences the Bible, reverences the Lord. The man who reads and studies his Bible carefully is a man who is constantly in touch with Jesus Christ. When a man's love for Jesus Christ grows cold, he invariably neglects his Bible.

A friend of mine, a Christian surgeon, has the following sentence written in the flyleaf of his Bible: "This Book will keep you from sin, and sin will keep you from this Book." If we Christians were as diligent in studying our Bibles as the communists are in studying Karl Marx, we would set the world on fire!

The Master told people of His day that they went astray because of their ignorance of the Bible.

Jesus answered and said unto them, Ye do err, not knowing the scriptures, nor the power of God. – Matthew 22 : 29.

Obviously there are different ways of studying the Bible, but to my mind the most effective method is that of committing the actual text of Scripture to memory. There are a few people who are able to shut themselves up for two or three hours each day and study individual Bible words in the original Hebrew or Greek, but for the majority of us this type of study is out of the question. However, the average Christian person could, with a little self-denial, devote twenty minutes each day to memorising. The man who uses this method of study is compelled to meditate on the Bible. His soul is nourished; his faith is increased; his love for God is deepened, and what is more he is preparing himself for effective Christian service both in personal witness and public speaking. Have you ever noticed how readily our Lord quoted Moses, the Psalms, and the Prophets. The Acts and Epistles leave us in no doubt that the Apostles also learned Scripture by heart.

It is clear from Psalm 119, often referred to as the 'Bible Psalm' that David believed in scripture memorising:

> Wherewithal shall a young man cleanse his way? by taking heed thereto according to Thy Word. With my whole heart have I sought thee: O let me not wander from thy commandments. Thy Word have I hid in mine heart, that I might not sin against thee. . . . I will delight myself in Thy statutes: I will not forget Thy Word. – Psalm 119: 9, 10, 11, 16.

I met a wonderful Christian man who had been a prisoner during the war, and for many months he was shut up in solitary confinement, and apart from a rough bed and chair he had nothing in his cell but his Bible. He made full use of the time, learning complete books by 'rote', and became one of the best Bible students I have ever met.

Alas, today's students spend little time in memory training. Undoubtedly in the past memorising was over emphasized, sometimes to the detriment of understanding, but is this any reason why it should be dropped entirely?

Winston Churchill was once asked: "Which of all the things you learnt at school did you find most helpful in later life?" Without any hesitation he answered: "The gems of literature which I memorised."

To store the mind with the Word of God is to improve one's powers of wisdom, reasoning, and judgment. Plato once said: "Knowledge is but to remember."

Don't be deceived by the myths that memory is an inherited ability, or that it is too late for adults to start memorising. When Paderewski was a boy he found it impossible to memorise music. He could retain pages of poetry after a few readings, and could play three games of chess at once with boards of competing adults out of his sight in another room, but music was a blank to him until, at the age of 15, he found a teacher who for the first time was able to make him see the musical meaning of a section, and when once he really understood the meaning of music, he was able to memorise entire symphonies.

Let me plead with Christian young people still in your teens or twenties, to store your memory with the actual words of the Bible and they will be with you for life. These great words of wisdom and power will get into your system, and will become the woof and warp of your very nature. You will never forget them.

In times of loneliness, frustration, tedium, sickness, weakness

Search the Scriptures

or sleeplessness it is of immense value to be able to quote slowly to oneself the Psalms of David, the utterances of the Prophets, the writings of the Apostles, and not least the words of our Lord Himself.

Every Christian should read carefully and meditate prayerfully upon a passage of the Bible each day, using the same questions suggested in the verse-by-verse study.

Search the scriptures; for in them ye think ye have eternal life: and they are they which testify of me. – John 5: 39.

They [the Bereans] received the word with all readiness of mind, and searched the scriptures daily, whether those things were so. – Acts 17: 11.

Whether you are a well-known minister, or a new convert, if you want to be pleasing to God and a blessing to others, discipline yourself in mastering the actual text of Holy Scripture – not books about the Bible, but the Bible itself, or "the sincere milk of the Word" as Peter calls it (1 Peter 2: 2).

What to Learn

Every intelligent Christian should be able to quote, without book, the ten commandments, the twenty-third Psalm, Isaiah 53, large sections, if not all, of the Sermon on the Mount, the better-known parables of our Lord, and 1 Corinthians 13. Why not start off by mastering these passages?

But do start memorising a complete book as soon as you feel able. Select first your favourite gospel, then move on to the Epistle which helps you most. Decide before you start which version of the Bible you plan to memorise. Don't start off in one and move to another or the result will be chaos! In the midst of every-day pressures, time is often quite a problem. Again, most people find that the early morning hour is the best. Set aside a clear twenty minutes each day – ten minutes for revision – five minutes for learning the verse of the day, and five minutes for reading aloud.

One of the commonest mistakes that Christian people make is that they think in terms of 'studying the *Bible*'. The Bible is not a book, but a library of sixty-six books. Moreover, each of these books is highly condensed. One short verse of holy Scripture contains more truth than any man-made theological tome. Therefore, take one book at a time, and if necessary major on that one book for three or five years. It is better to be well acquainted with one book of the Bible than to have merely a smattering of knowledge of each of the sixty-six books.

Personally, I am indebted to a retired missionary, the late Mrs. W. W. McLean, for putting me on to Bible memorisation. She told me: "While I was preparing for the mission field I was anxious to take to my new sphere of service a clear and complete picture of the Master, so I set to work and learned Mark's Gospel by heart."

For many years it has been my practice to learn one verse each day, concentrating each Sunday on revision. No, I cannot quote all the books that I have memorised – I find it easier to quote those which I memorised in my twenties than those which I have memorised in the last three years.

When Nicholas Ridley (1500–1555) was leaving his beloved Pembroke Hall, Cambridge, he wrote: "Farewell Pembroke Hall, of late mine own College, my cure and my charge! . . . In thy orchard (the walls, butts, and trees, if they could speak, would bear me witness) I learned without book almost all Paul's Epistles, yea, and I ween all the Canonical Epistles save only the Apocalypse. Of which study, although in time a great part did depart from me, yet the sweet smell thereof, I trust, I shall carry with me into heaven: for the profit thereof I think I have felt in all my life-time ever after."

It is extremely unwise to attempt to learn too many verses at a time. Some who have a great aptitude for learning might be able to manage three verses a day, whilst others find their capacity is limited to three verses a week. Why not do a little experimenting before you draw up rules for yourself. If you take up learning one verse a day, you will cover the average length chapter in a month, and in a very short while you will have mastered a complete book. There are more than 31,000 verses in the Bible, and if you take one verse each day, it will take you eighty-five years to memorise from Genesis to Revelation, so you had better get weaving!

And now a few practical suggestions as to the know-how of memorising. The key words are READ – THINK – LISTEN – LOOK – REVISE.

I. Read

Most books, and this certainly includes the Bible, exist primarily to be read. A careful reading is the best preparation for effective learning, especially if the Scripture is read out loud. Paul gave Timothy good advice to which I have referred elsewhere:

Till I come, attend to the public reading of scripture. – 1 Timothy 4: 13.

Each day read aloud in the chapter or the book that you are memorising. Read slowly, concentrating carefully on the meaning of the passage. Never attempt to read the Bible quickly. If you are a busy person, read ahead just one chapter each day. If today you are learning chapter 3 verse 14, read ahead from this as far as chapter 4: 13. If this preparation is done carefully each day, by the time you reach chapter 4: 13 you will probably find that you can quote it already.

II. Think

What physical exercise is to the body, memorising is to the mind. Many people suffering from mental depression tell me that

F

they have found complete release through exercising their mind by memorising a verse of the Bible early in the day. Never in any circumstances attempt to learn a verse, the meaning of which is not clear to you. Remember, the Bible is given to us not merely to be learnt, but to be understood and obeyed. Since the Scriptures were given by the inspiration of the Holy Spirit, the truth that they contain can only be understood by the revelation of the same Spirit. Before you attempt to memorise any verse, pray over it phrase by phrase, and word by word, and on bended knee seek divine light and understanding. Give God time.

As I have already said, the best commentary on the Bible is the Bible itself. Take pains to look up margin references. Read the verse in other versions, and when you have done this – not before – turn to a good commentary. Your motive in learning the Bible should not be merely to accumulate knowledge, but to know our Lord Himself, and to do His Will. You will find it much easier to learn a verse when once you understand its true meaning, and have applied it to everyday living.

Children often play 'The Memory Word Game'. The first child names an object 'The Sun', then the second says: 'The Sun reminds me of Heat', then the third 'And Heat reminds me of Cold' and so on, each object naturally reminding the players of another. This is merely an association of ideas. Now stop for a moment, and put *your* memory to the test. Read the following words slowly, looking for the connection between the words, then close the book and recite the words both forwards and backwards:

The Sun	Authors
Heat	Shakespeare
Cold	Stratford-on-Avon
Ice	English countryside
Winter	Wild flowers
Christmas	Spring
Presents	April showers
Shops	May flowers
Money	The Mayflower
Work	Pilgrim Fathers
Play	U.S.A.
Games	Sky scrapers
School	Clouds
Learning	The Sun
Books	

Now use this technique in learning the Bible. When memorising a Gospel story, the association of ideas is comparatively easy. One thing leads naturally to another. A question leads to a reply. An action calls for a comment. In the Psalms one thought usually rhymes or contrasts with another. In the Epistles often one argument leads on to another.

Many people find it comparatively easy to learn individual verses, but difficult to learn a passage or a sequence of verses. For this reason it is always safer to learn verses in pairs. Suppose you decide to learn one verse each day, you start by learning verse 1, tomorrow you revise verse 1 and learn verse 2 together, and next day you revise verse 2 and learn 3 together, and the following day revise verse 3 and learn 4 together, and so on. In this way you not only ensure mastering the sequence of verses, but at the same time you are revising the previous day's verse. Always bear in mind the connection between yesterday's verse and today's verse as in the 'Memory Word Game'.

III. Listen

Most of us can remember a tune, provided that we are able to hear it through again and again; and what is true of music is also true of a verse of Scripture. Repeat the verse you are learning out loud, together with the verse you memorised yesterday. Repeat the two verses slowly with expression, concentrating all the time upon their meaning. It is important that this should be done out loud. It may be necessary for you to repeat these two verses as many as twenty-five times, and in order that you may concentrate exclusively on the verses, you might find it helpful to count on your fingers and thumbs!

A Christian friend of ours, a busy housewife, has a tape recorder, and from time to time she will record her own voice reading slowly the chapter which she is currently learning, then when she is busy about her household chores, she will play back the tape, listening to it again and again.

IV. Look

It is said of Charles Haddon Spurgeon that he had a memory like a vice. As he read a heavy theological book his eyes never moved from left to right, they travelled down the middle of the page. He would then close the book, go into the pulpit, and quote what he had read verbatim. "It is not difficult," he said, "for in my mind's eye I can see the book. I simply read what I see." His mind was like a camera that took a picture of each page of the book. Spurgeon, of course, was outstanding, but there is no reason why ordinary folk like ourselves should not cultivate to some degree this photographic aspect of the memory. Because seeing helps us to memorise, *it is of the utmost importance* that you always use the same version and same edition of the Bible. This I have done since I became a Christian, and although I have never attempted to memorise the verse numbers, I usually find little difficulty in locating any particular verse, for I can "see" the exact page and position in my Bible where the verse is printed.

V. Revise

However good your memory may be, and remember it will improve with exercise, revision will always be necessary. The older you get, the more you will have to revise. What you learn in your teens you can quote in your forties, but what you learn in your forties you will have forgotten in your fifties unless you constantly revise. If you are working on one particular book, it's a good plan to revise the previous chapter each day. If you are today learning the 14th verse of the third chapter, then try to quote without book from the 14th verse of the second chapter. From time to time ask a friend to check you while you quote a chapter. Buy up every opportunity of quoting a chapter in public. I have lost count of the many people who have told me of the tremendous blessing they have received through hearing a chapter of the Bible quoted with meaning and expression rather than read directly from the Book.

For many years past, at the beginning of each month I draw up three lists for myself: (i) setting out the verses that I plan to memorise during the coming month; (ii) the revision that I am undertaking of books I have covered in previous years; (iii) my general Scripture reading. I think that every disciplined Christian should work out some simple system for himself concerning his memory studies.

To Summarise

May I now summarise the suggestions which I have set out above? Assuming that you are learning one verse a day, and that today you are to learn verse 14 of chapter 3:

1. Revise from chapter 2 verse 14 to chapter 3 verse 13.
2. Revise and learn chapter 3 verses 13 and 14 respectively.
3. Read ahead from chapter 3 verse 14 to chapter 4 verse 14.

It is easy to start with enthusiasm, but the only way to succeed is to discipline yourself to a daily routine. It will never be easy to learn the Bible or to pray. You will never *find* time – you must *make* time for this all-important task. The more you learn of the Bible the more you will enjoy it; the more you neglect it, the less you will want it.*

May I close this section on memorising by suggesting a prayer for you:

Thy hands have made me and fashioned me: give me understanding, that I may learn Thy commandments. – Psalm 119: 73.

III. DISCIPLINE IN READING

The Apostle Paul was a man of tremendous self-discipline. He writes about it in his letter to the Christians in Corinth:

I keep under my body, and bring it into subjection; lest that by any means, when I have preached to others, I myself should be a castaway. – 1 Cor. 9: 27.

It was his consuming devotion for the Lord Jesus that compelled him to say no to himself at every turn, and to submit to the discipline of his Lord; but Paul not only disciplined himself, but was constantly teaching and exhorting others to do the same. Read what he said to young Timothy:

So, my son, be strong in the grace that Jesus Christ gives.... Put up with your share of hardship as a loyal soldier in Christ's army. Remember: 1. That no soldier on active service gets himself entangled in business, or he will not please his commanding officer. 2. A man who enters an athletic contest wins no prize unless he keeps the rules laid down. – 2 Timothy 2: 1, 3, 4, 5.

The King's Regulations for His soldiers, and the rules of the Christian race involve not only physical discipline in such things as food, drink exercise, sleep, but also mental discipline. A vital part of the first and great commandment is:

Thou shalt love the Lord thy God with all thy mind. – Matthew 22: 37.

Whatsoever things are true, whatsoever things are honest, whatsoever things are just, whatsoever things are pure,

* A comprehensive booklet entitled *Learning the Bible by Heart* by Tom Rees is available, price 4d. (5c), postage extra, from The Bookroom, Hildenborough Hall, Otford Hills, Sevenoaks, Kent, England.

whatsoever things are lovely, whatsoever things are of good report; if there be any virtue, and if there be any praise, think on these things. – Phil. 4: 8.

Some of God's greatest saints have been constantly plagued with thoughts which were unjust, impure, and often intensely ugly, so don't be unduly disturbed if this is your experience too. Remember, temptation is not sin. Sin is yielding to temptation. Temptation is like an egg; leave it in the cold, and it will remain an egg; give it a warm place, and it will hatch into a bird. Saint Augustine, speaking of evil thoughts, said: "I cannot prevent the birds flying over my head, but I can stop them from building nests in my hair!"

Often the best method of defence is attack:

Be not overcome of evil, but overcome evil with good. – Romans 12: 21.

Therefore, one of the best ways of overcoming temptation in the realm of thought is to discipline your mind until every thought is controlled by the Lord.

Bringing into captivity every thought to the obedience of Christ. – 2 Corinthians 10: 5.

God in His infinite generosity has given to us not only His Holy Word but also many invaluable books filled with knowledge and wisdom to instruct and feed our minds. Consider once again the instructions that Paul gave to young Timothy:

Concentrate . . . on your reading and on your preaching and teaching. Never forget that you received the gift of proclaiming God's Word. . . . Give your whole attention, all your energies, to these things, so that your progress is plain for all to see. Keep a critical eye both upon your own life and on the teaching you give, and if you continue to follow the line I have indicated you will not only save your own soul but the souls of many of your hearers as well. – 1 Timothy 4: 13–16.

Yes, the Christian who would grow into spiritual maturity must discipline himself in Christian reading. He must concentrate on reading, giving his attention, and energy to it. First and foremost, he must give himself to a disciplined reading of the Bible itself, then Bible Commentaries, Christian biography, Church history, books on Christian evidence, devotional works to stir his heart, and theological books to instruct his mind.

Never waste your time, pollute your mind or endanger your

faith by reading authors who do not adhere wholeheartedly to the inspiration of Holy Scripture. The argument 'but you must know the other side' is often misleading and highly dangerous. Only a fool takes poison. A wise man eats only good, plain food. Concentrate on sound Biblical doctrine, and the moment you encounter heresy you will recognise it and know how to answer it. The bank cashier gets no instruction in identifying counterfeit money, but by daily handling thousands of good notes, he instantly recognises the false.

One of the main reasons why many Christians never witness for Christ in the presence of others is because of their ignorance of the Christian faith. They are quite unable to give a reason for the hope that is within them. – 1 Peter 3: 15.

If the average Christian spent as long studying the Bible as he did reading the newspaper, or reading good Christian books as he did reading cheap novels, he would be a far stronger Christian and a far better witness for his Lord.

IV. DISCIPLINE IN WORSHIP

"Can't a man be a good Christian without going to church?" The answer is an emphatic no – he can't! I suppose he can be a Christian of sorts, but a good Christian – certainly not! Needless to say there are many wonderful Christian people whose health, duties or circumstances prevent their worshipping with other believers regularly, but that's quite a different matter. The man who professes to love his family, but never bothers to go home is a humbug! The man who professes to be a keen rotarian, and shows no inclination to meet with fellow rotarians is a humbug, and the same goes for the man who professes to be a Christian, a follower of the Lord Jesus Christ, and has no desire to meet with his fellow Christians! Every country, society, institution and home has laws and rules which its members are expected to obey. The rules for the Christian are laid down clearly in his textbook, the Bible, which alone is his final court of appeal for faith and conduct. And here's one rule which no professing Christian has any right to disregard:

And let us not hold aloof from our church meetings, as some do. Let us do all we can to help one another's faith. – Hebrews 10: 25.

We have not only the plain command of Scripture, but also the example of our Lord:

And He came to Nazareth, where He had been brought up:

Beware of false prophets

and, *as his custom was,* he went into the synagogue on the
sabbath day. – Luke 4: 16.

If I call myself a disciple of Christ, then it is incumbent upon me
to do as He did in worshipping regularly.

Although the Master encouraged His disciples in the matter of
private prayer, the New Testament knows nothing of isolated
Christianity.

For where two or three are gathered together in My
Name, there am I in the midst of them. – Matthew 18: 20.

If a man is really a child of God, and knows Jesus Christ as his
Saviour and Lord, there will be no keeping him from meeting
with his fellow Christians for prayer, fellowship, and the Word of
God. He will meet with others not merely to *receive* help, but also
in order to *give* help. Our object in attending any Christian meeting
– be it church, or the Bible Cell – should be to *give*; worship,
thanksgiving, prayers, encouragement, gifts, service, and love. The
strength of a chain is in its weakest link, and the Christian who
cannot be relied upon to be present at worship, or the Bible Cell
slows the progress of the group, and weakens their corporate
witness.

It is of the utmost importance that the Church with which we
are identified is both Christ-centred, and Bible-based. Our Lord
tells us that we are to *beware* of false preachers – not to encourage
them!

Live chicks should never be put under dead hens! I have already written concerning the dangers of false prophets on page 138 and 139.

The mature Christian disciplines himself in identifying himself with and in supporting a lively Bible Church.

V. DISCIPLINE IN PERSONAL EVANGELISM*

A deep concern for the redemption of others is the hall-mark of spiritual life.

We always regard the Apostle Paul as a man full of the joy of the Lord. Wasn't he constantly exhorting others to:

Rejoice in the Lord alway: and again I say, Rejoice. – Phil. 4: 4.

yet the Apostle of joy was constantly burdened. He wept over his unbelieving kinsmen. Their being lost caused him great heaviness and continual sorrow (Romans 9: 1–3; 10: 1).

To be effective, as I have already said, our praying and witnessing must be concentrated. We should not pray vaguely for the salvation of "all those who are lost", but rather specifically – "O God, help me to lead my brother Jack to Thee". We should not be thinking in terms of mass evangelism, but rather concentrate our energies on winning the confidence, and bearing witness to the family next door, or to the man who works on the next bench to me in the factory. Most of us would rather hear our Lord say: "Go ye into all the world and preach the gospel" (Mark 16: 15) than "Go home to thy friends, and tell them how great things the Lord hath done for thee" (Mark 5: 19).

At the risk of wearying you, Mr. Reader, I want to say yet again, there is no quick or easy method of winning men for Christ.

If a man wants to grow flowers he doesn't hire a helicopter and scatter flower seed over the countryside. He goes out into his garden, prepares the soil, and then with love and care plants his seeds. Alas, too many Christian people prefer to wait for the helicopter than get down to the backaching job of gardening!

Mass production is all very well on the factory floor, but true evangelism calls for the skill and patience of the craftsman. It is far easier to concentrate on 'the mass media' than to get involved with the couple in deep spiritual need who live down the street.

When writing of Bible Cells at prayer, I suggested that each

* The author has prepared a comprehensive list of books and booklets, which he recommends, on the subject of Personal Evangelism. This list may be obtained, price 1s. 6d. (20c), postage extra, from The Bookroom, Hildenborough Hall, Otford Hills, Sevenoaks, Kent, England.

Christian, under God's guidance, should write the names of not less than six, and not more than twenty, individuals or families, and keep the list privately in his Bible, concentrating his prayers, love, and friendship on these people, seeking to lead them to Christ, at the same time inviting other Christians to covenant in prayer for their conversion. This type of evangelism calls for rigid personal discipline.

This is the Biblical and effective method of evangelism. It is how our Lord Himself worked, and how He taught His Apostles to work. Study carefully John chapter 1, verses 35–51 and see how God Himself introduced John the Baptist to Christ; the Baptist introduced Andrew; Andrew introduced Peter; Peter introduced Philip, and Philip introduced Nathanael.

VI. DISCIPLINE IN GIVING

A sure way of gauging a man's love for Christ is by the way he spends his money.

Money is powerful, it can do much; it can purchase property, pleasure, influence and power. A man's money represents himself, his time, his energy, and his skill. A mature Christian must learn to be disciplined in the way in which he spends his money. If, as some people imagine, it is unspiritual to talk about money, then the Bible must be a mighty unspiritual Book, for it is always talking about it!

Here's a good subject for your Bible Cell to study: 'The Right Use of Money'.

Paul had a tremendous lot to say about money. On one occasion, as I have already pointed out, he was deeply moved by the distress of his fellow Christians in Jerusalem who, largely through lack of money, were on the verge of starvation. I am sure the Apostle prayed about it, but he did far more. He opened a Famine Relief Fund and appealed to his fellow Christians everywhere for financial help. He wrote to the Church in Corinth:

> Now as far as the Fund for Christians in need is concerned, I should like you to follow the same rule that I gave to the Galatian Church. On the first day of the week let everyone put so much by him, according to his financial ability, so that there will be no need for collections when I come. – 1 Cor. 16: 1–2.

The Apostle was disappointed with the response to this appeal, and followed it up with another which is a classic on Christian stewardship which should be studied carefully by every intelligent

Christian. It is found in 2 Corinthians chapters 8 and 9. Like several passages in the Corinthian Epistles it is hard to understand in the authorised King James' version. J. B. Phillips is particularly clear; read it and study it carefully.

Why Give God our Money?

There are countless reasons why Christian people should give of their money to God, but let me here name but seven.

1. We should give our money to God because He is the Giver of all things.

> All things come of Thee, and of thine own have we given thee. – 1 Chron. 29: 14.

Our time, our energy, our talents, our health, our skill, life itself are all the gifts of God.

> But thou shalt remember the Lord thy God: for it is he that giveth thee power to get wealth. – Deut. 8: 18.

A certain percentage of all our income should therefore be set aside exclusively for God as an acknowledgment of His bounty.

2. We should give our money to God because He commands us to do so.

> Whosoever is of a willing heart, let him bring it, an offering of the Lord; gold, and silver, and brass. – Ex. 35: 5.

A mature Christian, out of love for Jesus Christ, gives sacrificially not only of his time, talents, and energy, but also of his pounds, shillings, and pence.

3. We should give our money to God because He has redeemed us.

> What? know ye not that . . . ye are not your own? For ye are bought with a price: therefore glorify God in your body. – 1 Cor. 6: 19, 20.

We belong to God, not only by creation, but by redemption. Because Christ has died for me, I belong to Him entirely – not only what I am, but also what I possess. Once purchased, a slave and his possessions are the exclusive property of his master.

> The silver is mine, and the gold is mine, saith the Lord of hosts. – Haggai 2: 8.

4. We should give our money to God for the blessing and development of our own souls.

Remember the words of the Lord Jesus, how he said, It is more blessed to give than to receive. – Acts 20: 35.

Here, straight from the lips of our Lord Himself we have the secret of happiness. Happiness is to be found in giving. Our human hearts rebel against this doctrine, but the only way of proving its truth is by putting it to the test. Covetous people are miserable people; generous people are joyous people.

Then the people rejoiced, for that they offered willingly, because with perfect heart they offered willingly to the Lord: and David the king also rejoiced with great joy. – 1 Chron. 29: 9.

Great possessions prevent many from entering the Kingdom of God,

How hardly shall they that have riches enter into the kingdom of God! – Luke 18: 24.

and also prevent those who have entered from being fruitful in the Kingdom of God.

And these are they which are sown among thorns; such as hear the word, and the cares of this world, and the deceit-fulness of riches, and the lusts of other things entering in, choke the word, and it becometh unfruitful. – Mark 4: 18, 19.

Yes, regular, disciplined giving is just as important to spiritual development as regular worship, prayer, and Bible study. God blesses people who give to Him. Nothing blurs a man's spiritual vision like meanness. Nothing sharpens his perception like generous, disciplined giving.

5. We should give our money to God because He regards each gift as a token of our love.

For God so loved the world that He gave. – John 3: 16.

The covetous heart clings to what it has, and grasps for more, whilst the loving heart gives what it has, and seeks more to give. The communist doctrine is 'Share what you have with me', whilst the Christian doctrine is 'Let me share what I have with you'.

I should like it [your gift] to be a spontaneous gift, and not money squeezed out of you by what I have said . . . . Let everyone give as his heart tells him, neither grudgingly nor under compulsion, for God loves the man whose heart is in his gift. – 2 Cor. 9: 6, 7.

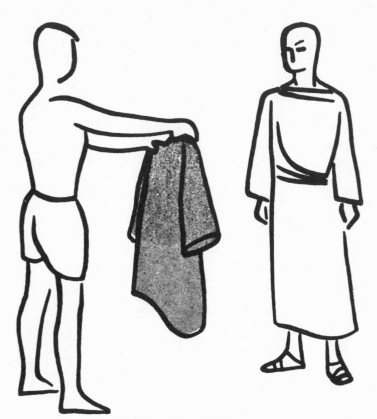

Naked, and ye clothed me

6. We should give our money to God because of the desperate
need of a suffering, lost world.

> Then shall the King say unto them on his right hand, Come,
> ye blessed of my Father, inherit the kingdom prepared for
> you from the foundation of the world. For I was an
> hungred, and ye gave me meat: I was thirsty, and ye gave
> me drink: I was a stranger, and ye took me in: naked, and
> ye clothed me: I was sick, and ye visited me: I was in
> prison, and ye came unto me. . . . Inasmuch as ye have done
> it unto one of the least of these my brethren, ye have
> done it unto me. – Matt. 25: 34–36, 40b.

God is not interested in our money for the sake of money, but .
for what it can do. Our money, dedicated to God, can train, equip,

and send forth men and women of the right calibre to proclaim His Word at home and overseas.

Our money, dedicated to Him, will enable missionary societies to enlist the services of first-class doctors, sisters and nurses, to go forth in His Name, to heal the sick and cleanse the lepers. Our money dedicated to Him, can provide food for the hungry, clothes for the naked, homes for the destitute.

7. We should give our money to God because He has given so sacrificially to us.

> He . . . spared not His own Son, but delivered Him up for us all. – Rom. 8: 32.

> Freely ye have received, freely give. – Matt. 10: 8.

When we realise that it was for us that God gave His Son; when we fully understand that it was for us that Christ shed His precious blood, then we will also want to give not only what we are, but also what we have to Him.

Although Paul uses many strong arguments as to why the Christians in Corinth should add generosity to their existing graces, his strongest argument was that of God's generosity towards them:

> For ye know the grace of our Lord Jesus Christ, that, though he was rich, yet for your sakes he became poor, that ye through his poverty might be rich. . . . Thanks be unto God for his unspeakable gift. – 2 Cor. 8: 9; 2 Cor. 9: 15.

The Cancer of Covetousness

Although there are innumerable reasons why we should give to God, there is but one basic reason why we do not give, and this can be named in one word – covetousness!

Covetousness is a greed of wealth with a view to hoarding; it is a strong desire to grasp that which belongs to another. Let us never forget that covetousness is SIN.

> Thou shalt not covet thy neighbour's house, thou shalt not covet thy neighbour's wife, nor his man servant, nor his maid servant, nor his ox, nor his ass, nor any thing that is thy neighbour's. – Ex. 20: 17.

Alas, covetousness is one of the commonest sins among Christian people. The Lord Himself said comparatively little about the sins of murder, adultery, lying and blasphemy, yet repeatedly warned us against the sin of covetousness.

Take heed, and beware of covetousness: for a man's life con-
sisteth not in the abundance of the things which he
possesseth. – Luke 12: 15.

Nothing distorts a Christian's vision of Christ so effectively as
covetousness.

The love of money is a root of all kinds of evil. – 1 Tim.
6: 10 (R.V.).

I have said that the Christian man who is too busy to pray is too
busy. I would add that the Christian man who cannot afford to
give to God is living beyond his income.

The Burning Question

Now exactly what proportion of his income should the disciplined Christian give to God? Obviously we should not give to
such an extent that we are no longer able to provide adequately
for those who depend upon us.

But if any provideth not for his own, and specially his
own household, he hath denied the faith, and is worse than
an unbeliever. – 1 Tim. 5: 8 (R.V.).

Those who give more than they should are rare indeed. Most
of us give too little.

But should we not give 'as and when we feel led' or 'as our
hearts are moved'? No, that is dangerous doctrine. Are we to
pray, read the Bible, go to church, and keep the commandments

The tithe . . . is the Lord's

by the same rule? Must the work of God depend upon our changing emotions or upon the eloquence of a deputation speaker?

Whilst the maximum amount we give to God is very much a personal problem that each of us must decide for himself, the minimum amount we are to give presents no problem whatsoever, for God has laid down a certain and clear guide for us in His Word. We are each to set aside a minimum of one-tenth of our income for Him and His work.

No matter whether our income is in the form of a wage, salary, stipend, profit, interest, dividend, or pocket money, ten cents in every dollar, £10 in every hundred belong to God.

The factory worker who earns £10 per week gives £1, and the schoolboy who receives 10s. pocket money gives 1s., and in the eyes of God the schoolboy's tithe is as valuable as that of the factory worker. God does not look so much at what we give, but rather at what we keep back for ourselves.

In Bible language a tithe is simply a tenth part, and the practice of giving a tenth is known as 'tithing'.

Many professing Christians have not even heard of tithing. Others think it is part of the Law of Moses, and therefore does not apply to New Testament Christians; but of course, the Bible is full of tithing, and what is more, it was practised not only by the New Testament Church, but also by the Patriarchs centuries before the Law was given to Moses.

As loyal citizens of an earthly kingdom recognise the right of their Sovereign to levy taxes on them, so we as citizens of Heaven must recognise the right of our King to His tithes.

It must be emphasised that the tithe is merely the basic amount which God claims for Himself. We do not start to give until we have paid our tithes.

Tithing is mentioned in the Bible as far back as Abraham:

And he (Abraham) gave him (Melchizedek) tithes of all. – Gen. 14: 18–20.

The timeless principle of tithing was naturally incorporated by God into the Law of Moses. Every tenth animal born was set aside for the Lord. Corn, wine, fruit, vegetables, and even herbs and spices were all meticulously tithed.

And all the tithe of the land, whether of the seed of the land, or of the fruit of the tree, is the Lord's: it is holy unto the Lord. – Lev. 27: 30.

The exact wording is important – it does *not* say 'All the tithes shall be given to the Lord'. It is not so much a command as a statement of fact: "The tithe . . . is the LORD's: it is holy unto the LORD." Whether the tithe was paid or withheld did not alter the fact that it belonged to the Lord.

It is significant that the only thing for which our Lord ever commended the Scribes and Pharisees was on account of their tithing – thus setting His seal of approval on the practice.

> Ye pay tithe of mint and anise and cummin . . . these ought ye to have done. – Matt. 23 : 23.

There were many Hebrew Christians in the Church at Corinth who from their earliest years had been trained to give one-tenth to the Lord, and there is little doubt that they understood perfectly what Paul had in mind when he wrote:

> Now concerning the collection. . . . Upon the first day of the week let every one of you lay by him in store, as God hath prospered him. – 1 Cor. 16: 1, 2.

Students of Church history tell us that tithing has been practised widely in the Christian Church since New Testament days.

The principle of tithing is timeless. It is for every man in every age and dispensation. It was neither instituted by the dispensation of law nor terminated by the dispensation of grace. It was neither given by Moses nor repealed by Jesus Christ.

Love is the fulfilling of the Law

Tithing was both incorporated into the Law of Moses and into the New Testament Church.

The principles of the Sabbath and tithing are both timeless. The Lord's day and the Lord's tithe stand or fall together.

> Yes, thank God we . . . are not under the law, but under grace. – Rom. 6: 14.

therefore the giving of our money and time is no longer a matter of legality and bondage, but rather of privilege and joyful experience.

If the Hebrews, compelled by Law, gave one-tenth, how can we, constrained by Grace, give one mite less?

> What then? shall we sin, because we are not under the law, but under grace? God forbid. – Rom. 6: 15.
>
> Love is the fulfilling of the Law. – Rom. 13: 10.

Robbing God

The Word of God through His servant Malachi concerning the cause of spiritual fruitlessness and material poverty should be studied carefully:

> Will a man rob God? Yet ye have robbed me. But ye say, Wherein have we robbed thee? In tithes and offerings. Ye are cursed with a curse: for ye have robbed me, even this whole nation. Bring ye all the tithes into the storehouse, that there may be meat in mine house, and prove me now herewith, saith the Lord of hosts, if I will not open you the windows of heaven, and pour you out a blessing, that there shall not be room enough to receive it. – Mal. 3: 8–10.

Although these words were originally addressed to the House of Jacob, no intelligent, honest Christian can possibly escape the weight and power of their moral teaching.

To appreciate the force of these words we must bear in mind that in every age God claims the tenth part of His people's increase as His. The tithe does not *become* God's property when it is given, but it *is* His property whether we bring it to Him or keep it back for ourselves.

No, it was not that God's people had broken into His temple and robbed the Treasury. Theirs was no blatant sin of commission, but a respectable sin of omission. They had simply failed to yield to God that which belonged to Him.

There is more than one way of robbing a man. I can break into his shop and steal £50 from the till, or I can run up a bill for £50 and keep on postponing payment until he writes it off as a bad debt, but whether I break in and steal, or merely fail to pay my account, I am nevertheless robbing my neighbour.

If someone suggested that we should break into the church and steal the Sunday collection of £50, the idea would fill us with horror, yet many of us have over the past years, without a qualm of conscience, robbed God of a far greater sum, in failing to bring Him His tithes and offerings.

If we fail to give God that which He claims as His, we may prefer our sin to be called 'Unfaithful Stewardship' or 'Embezzlement', but no matter what we call it, God calls it robbery, and robbery it is. Paying tithes, to the Christian, is not a matter of generosity, but of honesty.

If you used to be a thief you must not only give up stealing, but you must learn to make an honest living, so that you may be able to give to those in need. – Ephes. 4: 28.

Covetousness is the root cause of our robbery. What anger is to murder, and what lust is to adultery, covetousness is to robbery. Yes, that insidious sin of covetousness causes us to rob our Creator Who in generosity and grace gave His Son to die for us.

The plain fact is that some of us love money more than we love God.

No slave can serve two masters: for either he will hate the one, and love the other; or else he will hold to the one, and despise the other. Ye cannot serve both God and money. – Matt. 6: 24.

The Faithful Steward

There is, of course, a very real sense in which we should give 100 per cent. of our money to God. Both the Bible and our love for Christ teach us that we are answerable to Him not only for one-tenth of our income, but for ten-tenths. The man who imagines that because he has paid his tithe to God he is therefore at liberty to squander the remaining nine-tenths as he will, has no conception of Christian tithing and stewardship.

In this matter of giving we must be both realistic and honest, otherwise our would-be spiritual arguments may become merely an excuse either for covetousness or bad stewardship. When the man who argues "All my money belongs to God" is faced with an appeal to give, he can do one of two things. Either he can give his entire assets – cash and savings (why not? every penny belongs to God!), or he can give nothing (why should he give? – every penny already belongs to God!).

The Bible is perfectly clear. Although God holds me responsible for 100 per cent. of my money, I am to set aside a proportion of my income, not less than one-tenth regularly each week, to be used exclusively for His work.

This proportion is to be kept entirely separate from that which I spend on myself and family. I am not to budget first for myself and my family, and then give to God the fragments that remain (if any), but as His steward I must first budget a fixed proportion of my income for Him, and then cut my personal and family budget according to that which is left.

Do not hesitate to commence tithing because you feel you can't afford it. Is God asking too much in demanding His tithe? No, the tithe is only a reasonable sacrifice.

A Christian professional man and his wife came and talked to me about tithing.

"It's no good," he said, "I should love to be able to give my tithe to the Lord, but the plain fact is I am already committed right up to the hilt."

Beware of covetousness

But after discussing the matter frankly, we discovered that for some years he and his wife had been living beyond their means in trying to keep up with the Jones. The house they lived in was larger and more luxurious than was necessary. His wife would have looked just as nice if she had spent a little less on clothes, cosmetics, and hairdressing. The annual family holiday was truly fabulous and cost a small fortune. And so it was inevitable that someone somewhere had to suffer. What was it to be? Did they suffer? Certainly not! Did their children suffer? No, they took good care of them! Was it the tradespeople who suffered? Emphatically not! As good Church people they must pay their bills! Well, was it the Building Society? No! Was it the credit company who owned the TV and the family car? No, those things *had* to be paid for. Was it the Bank? Did they forge cheques or stage a hold-up at the Bank? No, that would be highly irregular! No, none of these folk suffered. They neither robbed themselves, nor the tradesmen, nor the credit company, nor the Bank – they simply did what thousands of others do – they just robbed God by failing to pay their tithes. And whose fault was it that they were compelled to rob God in this way? Obviously it was entirely their own fault. It was a matter of bad stewardship caused by pride and covetousness.

This couple did what many others ought to do. They prayed over their financial problems, then settled down together and worked out their exact income, and budgeted carefully their expenditure, economising here and there to enable them to open and operate a proper tithe account.

Undoubtedly one of the greatest weaknesses of the evangelical Christian Church is that for the most part we are undisciplined not only in our devotional lives, but in our stewardship of time and money.

. . . And Running Over

Under the old covenant God promised material prosperity to those who brought their tithes and offerings to Him.

> Honour the Lord with thy substance, and with the firstfruits of all thine increase: so shall thy barns be filled with plenty, and thy presses shall burst out with new wine. – Prov. 3: 9, 10.

Although the New Testament does not clearly promise material prosperity to those who give, the blessing is nevertheless implied. Consider the words of Jesus:

181

But seek ye first the kingdom of God, and his righteousness; and all these things (food, drink, clothes) shall be
added unto you. – Matt. 6: 33.

Give, and it shall be given unto you; good measure,
pressed down, and shaken together, and running over . . .
for with the same measure that ye mete withal it shall be
measured to you again. – Luke 6: 38.

St. Paul in his great financial appeal to the Corinthians reminds
us that if we honour God in giving, He in turn is able to give to
us so that we will have not only enough for ourselves, but enough
to give again.

After all, God can give you everything that you need, so that
you may always have sufficient both for yourselves, and for
giving away to other people. – 2 Cor. 9: 8.

I believe that there are many Christian individuals, families,
and businesses with financial problems who would experience a
new prosperity if they would honour God in their financial affairs
by tithing.

During the past few years I have discussed the matter of tithing
with hundreds of individual Christian people all over the world,
and all of these people, without exception, have borne witness to
the fact that after they started tithing they found that the remaining
nine-tenths went much further than the ten-tenths did before they
started honouring God in this way.

You can't afford to tithe? You can't afford *not* to tithe!*

Someone once said that when a man starts tithing he will be
surprised at seven things:

1. At his unspeakable joy and satisfaction.
2. At his spiritual development and growth.
3. At his growing desire to give yet more.
4. At his increased sympathy for those in need.
5. At his growing sense of responsibility concerning the
   remaining nine-tenths.
6. At how very far the remaining nine-tenths will go.
7. At his stupidity for not starting to tithe sooner.

For we brought nothing into this world, and it is certain
we can carry nothing out. – 1 Timothy 6: 7.

* A comprehensive book on Christian Stewardship, entitled *Money Talks* by
Tom Rees, is available, price 2s. (25c), postage extra, from The Bookroom,
Hildenborough Hall, Otford Hills, Sevenoaks, Kent, England.

Nothing in . . . nothing out

VII. DISCIPLINE IN SERVING

Before the Reformation the emphasis was all on good works whilst faith was largely overlooked, but today in many Christian circles the pendulum has swung to the other extreme; the emphasis is all on faith, whilst good works, if not positively frowned upon, are almost totally forgotten; but the Scriptures maintain the perfect balance.

> For by grace are ye saved through faith . . . *not of works* . . . for we are *His workmanship*, created in Christ Jesus *unto good works*, which God hath before ordained that we should walk in them. – Ephes. 2: 8–10.

No, we are not saved *by* our good works, but only by the good workmanship of Christ. However, we must never forget that we are saved *to* good works – not any good works, but specific good works which God in His wisdom has planned for us.

Again and again in his Epistles Paul writes first about the Christian faith, and then about the Christian way of life. For instance, in his Epistle to the Romans, he devotes the first eleven chapters to the Christian gospel, and then suddenly in chapter 12 brings his readers face to face with the importance of practical Christian living. Again, his Letter to the Ephesians is divided quite naturally into two parts: the first three chapters deal with belief; the last three with behaviour. We find the same balance in the teaching of our Lord Himself.

Christian good works most certainly include spiritual exercise

Pure religion and undefiled

and activity such as Prayer, Bible Study, Worship, and Witnessing, but no one can read the New Testament with an open mind and gain the impression that Christian people should be engaged exclusively in religious and spiritual activities. Ponder carefully the following Scriptures:

Let your light so shine before men, that they may *see your good works*, and glorify your Father which is in heaven. – Matt. 5: 16.

As for the rich in this world, charge them . . . *to do good, to be rich in good deeds*, liberal and generous, thus laying up for themselves a good foundation for the future. – 1 Tim. 6: 17–19.

Jesus Christ; Who gave himself for us, that he might redeem us from all iniquity, and purify unto himself a peculiar people, *zealous of good works*. – Titus 2: 13, 14.

Let us consider one another to provoke unto love and to *good works*. – Heb. 10: 24.

Pure religion and undefiled before God and the Father is

this, *To visit the fatherless and widows in their affliction.* – James 1: 27.

What doth it profit, my brethren, though a man say he hath faith, and have not works? can (that) faith save him? If a brother or sister be naked, and destitute of daily food, and one of you say unto them, Depart in peace, be ye warmed and filled; notwithstanding ye give them not those things which are needful to the body; what doth it profit? Even so faith, if it hath not works, is dead, being alone. – James 2: 14–17.

Whereas they speak against you as evildoers, they may by *your good works*, which they shall behold, glorify God in the day of visitation. – 1 Peter 2: 12.

But if any one has the world's goods and sees his brother in need, yet closes his heart against him, how does God's love abide in him? – 1 John 3: 17.

Rich in Good Deeds

It is perfectly clear from these, and many other Scriptures, that Christ died for us not only that we might be redeemed from evil works but that we might be constantly and zealously engaged in good works, and that these good works are connected primarily with "those things which are needful to the body". We are to give food to the hungry, drink to the thirsty, hospitality to the needy, friendship to the lonely, clothing to the destitute, practical help to the sick. We are to visit the prisoners, care for the orphans, support the widows, share our earthly possessions with the poor, and open our homes to our neighbours. This is Christian love in action. This is following our Lord Who not only preached repentance, but "went about doing good" (Acts 10: 38).

I have been an itinerant preacher for many years, and have been entertained in countless Christian homes throughout the world, and I have noticed that people who really love the Lord Jesus are invariably deeply involved not only in evangelism, but also in ministering to the physical needs of others. Of course, the soul is more important than the body. The bread of life is of greater value than the baker's loaf. In Christian thinking, the spiritual must always have priority over the physical, but at the same time we must bear in mind that we can only communicate the spiritual through the physical. It is only through our works, not our words, that our faith can be seen and appreciated.

I was sick and ye visited me

A man may say, Thou hast faith, and I have works: shew
me thy faith without thy works, and I will shew thee my
faith by my works. – James 2: 18.

Now once again in this matter of good works many of us lack
personal discipline. The New Testament singles out at least four
groups of people to whom we as Christians should minister, both
in the physical and spiritual realms. They are: (i) the sick, (ii) the
bereaved, (iii) widows, orphans, and those in special need, (iv)
the lonely, especially elderly people. We all know people amongst
our immediate relatives and acquaintances who fall into one of
these groups. It is useless our merely 'feeling sorry' for people.
We must do far more; we must pray for them regularly and
earnestly, visit them, befriend them, and show them practical
Christian kindness and generosity.

You must not be vague. Give the matter prayerful consideration,
take pen and paper, and under the guidance of the Lord write

down the names of sick people, sad people, people in special need and elderly people, and purpose in your heart to bear their burdens with them by daily prayer, genuine Christian love, and practical kindness. Undoubtedly God will guide you to some who have little time for spiritual things, who are unattractive and selfish, and will never be able to repay you. But this again is all part of practical Christian discipleship.

> When you give a dinner or a banquet, do not invite your friends or your brothers or your kinsmen or rich neighbours, lest they also invite you in return, and you be repaid. But when you give a feast, invite the poor, the maimed, the lame, the blind, and you will be blessed, because they cannot repay you. – Luke 14: 12–14.

Not Words but Deeds

Now, having completed your list, commence praying daily for each person by name. Visit them regularly, giving of your love and friendship. Write to them when you are away on holiday; remember them specially on their birthdays and at Christmas. Find out what they are interested in, and for their sakes take an interest in it too. The world is just full of young people, adults, and old folk who are in desperate need of human love and friendship, but do be intensely practical.

> My little children, let us not love in word, neither in tongue; but in deed and in truth. – 1 John 3: 18.

When visiting elderly people, be a good listener. Ask for their advice. Have something interesting to tell them. Your latest joke may help, old people often enjoy a good laugh. Some will appreciate your help in housework, gardening, shopping, or your taking them to church in your car on Sunday.

When I was at the Parish church, Sevenoaks, one of my responsibilities was to visit the people in the Alms Houses. Sometimes when I was feeling under the weather spiritually I would call on these old folk, and share their burdens with them, only to find my own spirit was greatly cheered. I always gained far more than I gave.

You will find tremendous help and inspiration in a disciplined programme of practical good works. Don't be like the priest or the Levite who saw a needy man and passed by on the other side, but be like the good Samaritan who saw, had compassion, went to him, and got involved (Luke 10: 30–37).

Let us have no imitation Christian love. Let us have a genuine break with evil and a real devotion to good. Let us have real warm affection for one another as between brothers, and a willingness to let the other man have the credit. Let us not allow slackness to spoil our work and let us keep the fires of the spirit burning, as we do our work for God. Base your happiness on your hope in Christ. When trials come endure them patiently; steadfastly maintain the habit of prayer. Give freely to fellow-Christians in want, never grudging a meal or a bed to those who need them. And as for those who try to make your life a misery, bless them. Don't curse, bless. Share the happiness of those who are happy, and the sorrow of those who are sad. Live in harmony with each other. Don't become snobbish but take a real interest in ordinary people. – Romans 12: 9–16.

Men not Methods

In writing of methods of Bible Study, prayer, and evangelism, we must never for one moment overlook the fact that it is not methods, but men that God uses. What is more, the men that God uses need not necessarily be clever, but they must be clean.

> Behold, the Lord's hand is not shortened, that it cannot save. . . . But your iniquities have separated between you and your God. – Isaiah 59: 1, 2.

Members of a Cell may know their Bibles from Genesis to Revelation; they may be masters of every Biblical technique; they may be efficient and tireless workers, but if they are consciously trifling with sin and worldliness, all their knowledge, methods, efficiency, and labours will count for nothing. Their Bible studies will be lifeless, their prayers powerless, and their witness ineffective. God is more concerned with new men than with new methods. In Joshua's day there was no walled city, army, or nation could stand before God's people Israel while they walked with Him in obedience and holiness, but the sin of just one man, Achan, robbed Israel of its power, and brought a humiliating, crushing defeat.

Christian people shake their heads sadly over the godlessness, immorality, worldliness, and materialism which abounds in the world today, but alas, few realise that these insidious things have also infiltrated the Christian Church. Whilst the world is no longer conscious of sin, the Church is no longer conscious of worldliness.

If Christian people in a Bible Cell are to be blessed in their study of the Word; if they are to be effective in their prayers, and fruitful in their evangelism, then absolute priority must be given to holiness of life and Christlikeness of character. Our relatives and neighbours are in desperate need of the life-giving touch of the Son of God. Moreover, the Saviour is desperately anxious to seek and save the lost. Then if the lost need His salvation, and He is longing to save, why do we see so little of His saving grace? The answer to this question is to be found in the fact that God, for some wise purpose, limits Himself to working in and through His people. Our God is still a mighty Man of War, but His weapons are neither movements nor methods, but men. As God used His ancient people

Israel as His weapons of war, so today He is anxious to use common Christian people like you and me.

> Thou art my battle axe and weapons of war: for with thee will I break in pieces the nations, and with thee will I destroy kingdoms. – Jeremiah 51: 20.

I believe God's greatest need – yes, and the world's greatest need – is for men and women who are given over utterly to God, who seek to obey Him in things small and great; who will have done with lesser things, seeking the fullness of the Holy Spirit.

The British Forces lost everything at Dunkirk; weapons and equipment were all abandoned, only the soldiers themselves reached the shores of England. But no sooner had the men set foot on land than they were asking to be sent back again to France at once to face the foe. But such a thing was impossible. Why? Didn't the enemy need to be defeated? Indeed he did! Were not our men anxious to go back and fight? They certainly were! Then why were they not sent? The answer is obvious – they had no war weapons! Yet in that dark hour these brave yet helpless men cried: "Give us the tools and we will finish the job." And for nearly four long years they waited. God too is looking for weapons and tools, clean, sharp, and available – you and me!

> In a great house there are not only vessels of gold and of silver, but also of wood and of earth; and some to honour, and some to dishonour. If a man therefore purge himself from these, he shall be a vessel unto honour, sanctified, and meet for the Master's use, and prepared unto every good work. – 2 Timothy 2: 20, 21.

I have heard people pray that the Holy Spirit might move from house to house convicting men of sin, and converting them to Christ, but the Holy Spirit rarely, if ever, works independently of God's people. Only when my soul is blessed will others be blessed through me. Only as I am filled with God's Spirit will others know His Presence and feel His touch of power.

Vessels of gold, silver, wood and earth

Early one morning whilst conducting a mission in Northern Ireland, I was preparing the next day's message, when the following verse struck me with particular force.

And when He (the Holy Spirit) is come (unto you) (this is understood from the verse 7), He will reprove (convict) the world of sin. – John 16: 8.

When He is come (*unto you*) in all His fullness, the worldling will be convicted of his sin. I had often read this verse, but had never before seen the significance of the words 'unto you'. The next day I spoke on this verse, and shared with the people what God had given to me. The following morning brought a letter from my friend, Arthur Willis in Portsmouth. The letter carried a postscript: 'I have just been reading John 16, and have realised that it is only when the Holy Spirit is come "to you" will the world be convicted of sin.' In the same hour that God revealed this truth to my friend in southern England, He revealed it to me in Northern Ireland. I have never forgotten this lesson.

Amongst those who heard the message that God had given to me on John 16: 8 were two Christian young women. Walking home after the service one said to her friend:

"I have been a Christian for some years, but I really can't say that I have ever crowned Jesus Christ Lord of all in my life."

"Neither have I," said her friend, "but by His grace I mean to tonight."

That night, alone in their bedrooms, they both yielded themselves fully to Jesus Christ, seeking from Him the fullness of His Holy Spirit.

These two girls were employed in the same factory, and between them worked another girl who had no interest whatsoever in the things of God. The following morning neither of the Christian girls said a word concerning spiritual things, but suddenly the girl between them fell on her knees and started to pray aloud that God would forgive her sins and make her a true Christian. The power of the Holy Spirit in the unspoken witness of those two Spirit-filled young women was so great that their non-Christian friend was convicted of her sin, and truly converted to Christ.

We are privileged to live in thrilling days, days of unparalleled opportunity and challenge. Let us give ourselves – all we are, and all we have – body, soul, and spirit – to the Son of God Who gave His all for us. Let us purpose in our hearts that we will never grieve His Spirit, but walk with Him in obedience and faith, that His Name might be glorified in the blessing of His people, and the salvation of the lost.

Give me the faith which can remove
  And sink the mountain to a plain;
Give me the child-like praying love
  Which longs to build Thy house again;
Thy love, let it my heart o'erpower
And fill me from this very hour.

I would the precious time redeem,
  And longer live for this alone,
To spend, and to be spent, for them
  Who have not yet my Saviour known;
Fully on these my mission prove,
  And only breathe, to breathe Thy love.

My talents, gifts, and graces, Lord,
  Into Thy blessed hands receive,
And let me live to preach Thy word,
  And let me to Thy glory live;
My every sacred moment spend
  In publishing the sinners' Friend.

Enlarge, inflame, and fill my heart
  With boundless charity divine:
So shall I all my strength exert,
  And love them with a zeal like Thine;
And lead them to Thy open side,
  The sheep for whom their Shepherd died.

– Charles Wesley

A comprehensive list of books and booklets about Bible Cells, giving titles, authors, publishers, a description, and prices, is available, price 1s. 6d. (20c) post free from The Bookroom, Hildenborough Hall, Otford Hills, Sevenoaks, Kent, England.

General Index

THE HILDENBOROUGH BOOKLETS

Price 4d. (5c) each (4s. (50c) per dozen) postage extra

GOD WONDERED . . .

by

JEAN A. REES

Foreword by Mrs. Billy Graham

Many of the chapters in this book deal with the subject of Prayer and Intercession, and are ideally suited for groups when a chapter is read from a devotional book

Price 18s. 6d. ($2.50) (postage extra)

The above books, and all other Christian literature, may be obtained from The Bookroom, Hildenborough Hall, Otford Hills, Sevenoaks, Kent, England. (Remittance and postage with order, please.)